ALL ROADS LEAD TO NOWHERE

ALL ROADS LEAD TO NOWHERE

ALEXANDER SKIKOS

NEW DEGREE PRESS
COPYRIGHT © 2021 ALEXANDER SKIKOS
All rights reserved.

ALL ROADS LEAD TO NOWHERE

ISBN
978-1-63676-367-5   *Paperback*
978-1-63676-448-1   *Kindle Ebook*
978-1-63676-368-2   *Digital Ebook*

CONTENTS

ACKNOWLEDGMENTS		9
PROLOGUE		13
CHAPTER 1.	I HATE TALK SHOW DAY	21
CHAPTER 2.	WELCOME TO PARADISE	31
CHAPTER 3.	NO NAMES	39
CHAPTER 4.	NO TALKING	45
CHAPTER 5.	NO STOPPING	55
CHAPTER 6.	THE PYRAMID	65
CHAPTER 7.	INTO THE LABYRINTH	73
CHAPTER 8.	THE LABYRINTH	81
CHAPTER 9.	PARADISE CITY: NEW YORK	91
CHAPTER 10.	THE SHOW PART ONE	99
CHAPTER 11.	THE SHOW PART TWO	109
CHAPTER 12.	THE MAN IN THE PINK FLIP-FLOPS	121
CHAPTER 13.	CITY OF BLINDING TRASH	131
CHAPTER 14.	GOOD DOME	139
CHAPTER 15.	DREAMS ARE LIES WITH SUGAR	151
CHAPTER 16.	DO ALL DAYS START THIS BAD?	159
CHAPTER 17.	WARNING: THE HAPPY PLACE MAY INCLUDE CANNIBALS	167
CHAPTER 18.	OTHER LAND	175
CHAPTER 19.	PURPLE SMILES	181
CHAPTER 20.	THE BAD GUY	187
CHAPTER 21.	LIBERATION DAY	197

CHAPTER 22.	BIG DOGS	207
CHAPTER 23.	NO BETTER TIME THAN NOW	215
CHAPTER 24.	THE WRIGHT GANG	221
CHAPTER 25.	WHY ARE SMART PEOPLE SO DUMB?	231
CHAPTER 26.	RIVALS, FRIENDS, AND THE P.R.R.C.	241
CHAPTER 27.	MOONSHOTS AND OTHER DUMB DREAMS	249
CHAPTER 28.	DUST CLOUDS AND DEMONS	253
CHAPTER 29.	THE FACTORY PART ONE	259
CHAPTER 30.	THE FACTORY PART TWO	271
CHAPTER 31.	LOVE OR LUST PART ONE: THE DOGS	277
CHAPTER 32.	LOVE OR LUST PART TWO: FULL OF G.L.E.	283
CHAPTER 33.	LOVE OR LUST PART THREE: THE BLEEDING ROSE	293
EPILOGUE		297

ACKNOWLEDGMENTS

To the beta readers, I wanted to thank you all for taking a chance on me (yes, that's an ABBA reference). In all seriousness, thank you for taking the time to read what I sent, but also dealing with me asking, "Are you entertained?" and "Did you get that reference?" over and over again. Your embracing of my ideas and encouragement throughout this process really helped me along this journey.

To everyone who contributed to my IndieGoGo Campaign: Joyce Baker, Gabi Ballardo, Rohan Bhatt, Alle Cacchione, Chris Casciani, Jeff Collins, Ian Corbett, Earvin da Silva, Anthony Damore, Abel Daniel, Sami Fahid Daoud, Andrea Horvath, Autumn Inman, Eric Koester, Sarina Kong, Siobhan Lawlor, KJ Lee, Katie Luttringer, Rod and Tarik Naber, Ryan Nazari, Brandon Negranza, Ella Naylor, Nico Raymundo, Aaron Ross, John Samawi, Karam Samawi, Sam Samawi, Sana Samawi, Molly Saxelby, Theresa Simon, Greg Skikos, Ilana Skikos, Matt and Dana Skikos, Monica Skikos, Steve and Ida Skikos, Athena Snyder, Andrea Tai, Marissa Velez, Andrea Vlahos, Justin Vlahos, Mikaela Wentworth, Anne Whitaker, Dylan Yapp.

I want to shout out Athena Snyder, Andrea Horvath, and Ilana Skikos for taking the time to give detailed reports on each chapter. Your opinions were very clear and helpful. You did not hesitate to tell me if you did not like something. Anything. Even a single word. I can definitely see you all being editors in the future.

Also, shout out to Mikaela Wentworth. You sat with me for three hours and helped create the initial design for the map of the Paradise City. Anyone who can listen to me go on about a fictional apocalypse for three hours and come out sane deserves special praise.

But most of all, I want to thank my parents, Steve and Ida Skikos. You both have been there for me from the beginning of this journey all the way back in high school. You invested so much time into this story, listening to me ramble about what each character represents, what parts of the plot aren't working, and how the world will end for years. You took the time to actually get to know these characters, their world, and their journey. This book is as much mine as it is yours.

NDP Staffers:

Thanks to the New Degree Press team who helped make this book a reality. Special thanks to Eric Koester for creating this program and allowing me to join it, Marketing and Revisions Editor Alan Zatkow, Acquiring Editor Lauren Sweeney, and Developmental Editor Michael Bailey for helping develop my ideas into a thorough and cohesive story, and Gjorgji Pejkovski, the greatest cover designer (and cartographer) the world has ever known.

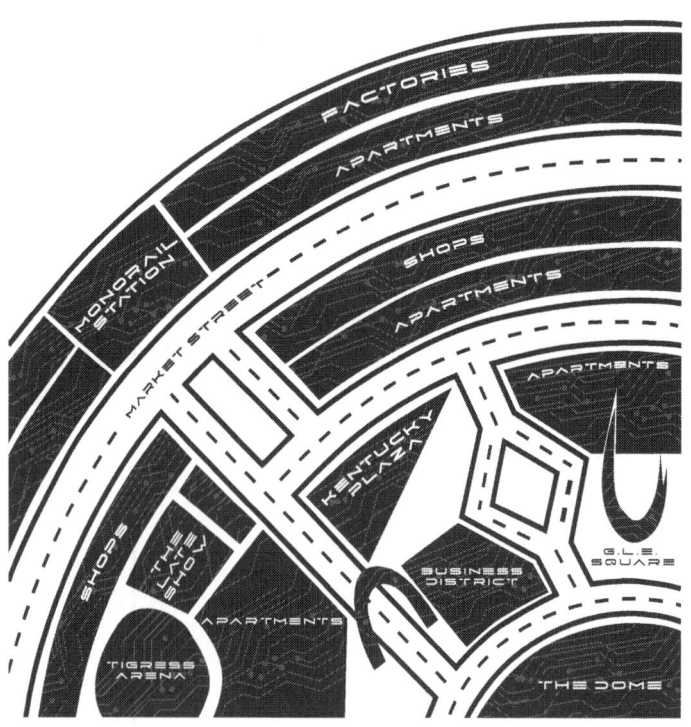

12 · ALL ROADS LEAD TO NOWHERE

PROLOGUE

PRESIDENT JIMMY MARSHALL
OCTOBER 10, 2052

Where's the spy?

I stare over the densely populated Iowa crowd. A never-ending field of tall grass encircles the mud pit my team cut for the citizens to stand in, creating an amphitheater. About 1,400 people push together in front of me, dressed in attire ranging from country and western to black tie. Some carry rifles strapped to their backs. The poor yield farmland tools: pitchforks, clubs, hoes, and others. All faces look concerned. All are sweating. Anxious. Anticipating good news. At least most are American.

Headlights from the surrounding black SUVs circle the mud, lighting the hot, muggy night. I reach into my coat pocket and feel my mother's deck of cards. Gripping them tightly, I take a deep breath. My legs shake behind the cheap splintering podium. My black dress shoes, scuffed from overuse, seem to melt into the poorly black-painted stage. My black slacks are filthy from the mud I had to slosh through to stand up here.

Luckily for me, no one can see my legs—only my head. So, I take my hand out of my coat pocket and force a stoic look onto my face to calm the crowd's anxiety. The singular camera seems to confront me as it shows my ugly reflection.

I look like a thug.

"The camera is on, sir. The nation is waiting." Leonardo Santos stares at me from the bottom of the stage to my left. His usual joyous smile has transformed to a beaten-down grin, barely making a wrinkle on his pale face. His eyes look down and seem lifeless. His black suit still has some blood on it, reminding me why I need to do this.

If we can save lives, it's not a loss.

We lost because they knew how greedy we are. By buying off the worst of us, they won, bombing us with our own arsenal. With complete control of our arsenal, what chance did we have? All we could do was run and watch.

Where is their spy? I look around for a man dressed in stereotypical American attire (a flannel, cowboy hat, jeans, and boots) but cannot spot him in this crowd. Too many men dress like that. *Maybe they're all spies.*

"It's okay, sir," Leo's nasally voice encourages. "I know they can take it."

We hid from the fires and the explosions, not because we were afraid but because we were selfish. That can no longer stand. Especially now, even if it condemns me to death.

Taking a deep breath, I begin. "My fellow citizens, I stand here today humbled by your efforts to salvage this country and maintain the integrity that has allowed us to thrive for so long. You have shown, not only to me and to the others around you, but have proven to yourselves that good character triumphs over any hardship that may come our way. You have once again demonstrated to the world what it truly means to be an American. You have stepped out of your comfort zones to help neighbors through the toughest our enemies, and even Mother Nature, have thrown at us. You have reached beyond your limits to help your fellow brothers and sisters in their times of need, and for that, I adore you."

The crowd applauds, then turns quiet as if they know what I'm about to say.

"We have entered an unprecedented era in our democracy. Throughout our country's history, never has our freedom been opposed so forcefully. Never has the conquest for power, led by our enemies to prove that democracies cannot work, been so aggressive. Well, I am here to inform you that today, I stand before you to ask you one question. What is the one thing they can't take from us?"

The crowd yells back in a wave of anger. I only make out a couple of chants.

"Our lives!" screams a lady.

"Freedom!" yells a man.

"Our guns!" bellows another.

I raise my hand, and the crowd quiets, and I say, "No. They can't take away our character. That's only something we can hand them. That's how we lose. If we give in to what the People's Republic of Russia and China want, we will lose this war. If we give in to their threats, to their terror, to their hysteria, we are no better than them. If we lose our character, if we gift away our hope, there is no chance we can win."

I raise my chin and strain as a confident smirk tears through my cracked and dry lips.

"But this is America. This is the land of the blue-collar man. The man who pulls himself up off the ground no matter how many times he gets knocked down. This is the land of opportunity, not waited on, but seized because we know damn well if an opportunity comes knocking, it's not coming back again. This is the land where we scratch and claw, where we get dirty because we do whatever it takes to win. This is the land where people don't go down without a fight.

We never have, and you're damn sure we never will. We will not give in to their pressures because it is not who we are. We are here for the long haul, ladies and gentlemen. They may believe they've won this war, but they should know better. Because nobody can truly beat an American."

The crowd in front of me erupts into fanatic cheers. People, even those in their formal attire, jump around in the mud, cheering as if their favorite football team has won the Super Bowl.

How long can I maintain this noble lie? I have undoubtedly sentenced myself, and even these people, to death, but to give a little hope to such depleted … it has to be worth it. I cannot have my citizens fearing every day, especially when our end is so close.

Despite the roaring applause and success of the speech, my legs still shake unsteadily.

This has to be worth it.

The red record light switches off on the camera in front of me.

Leo walks from behind and says, "I apologize for my bluntness, sir, but what the hell was that? You're not going to tell them we lost?"

I stare at Leo's pale face. His eyes dart from me to the crowd. Calmly I respond, "Leo, my father once told me of this idea called the noble lie. Socrates, who I assume you know, deemed it okay to lie as a ruler if it meant the peace in the city, or in our case, the nation, is well maintained."

"But, uh sir, you just condemned all of us to death! The P.R.R.C. …"

"We will have to deal with what comes, Leo. And I appreciate your concern for your own well-being, but put yourself in the position of these people. Would you rather die scared, looking over your shoulder for the rest of your life in a state of misery, waiting for the inevitable bullet to catch you, or die in a peaceful ignorance?"

Leo stares at me blankly. For a man with so much passion for salvaging what is left of society, he is too blinded by his self-preservation. I'm not yet sure if he is worthy of the programming.

After a moment of silence, Leo's phone buzzes. He pulls it out of his pocket. The light of the screen shines on his face. I study his expression, looking for any reaction. The barely visible freckles above his nose come together as he studies the message.

"There's been a problem with the construction of the Paradise City."

"Which one?"

"New York, sir. Seems like a couple of employees are quitting on us."

Sighing heavily, I say, "Ready the car. I'll be there in a moment."

"Yes, sir." Leo runs down the steps to my left and informs one of the officers.

As I follow him, one of my guards approaches. The jet-black robot wears a traditional black police uniform and has blue-lit eyes poking out of its emotionless steel face. Something is off. The officer is walking too fluidly, more humanlike. It's too short, maybe 5'7". Its strides are with a minor limp …

I reach for the Desert Eagle on my holster, but the man restrains me with an ironclad grip. He puts his other hand over my mouth and stuffs what feels like paper into it. He says to me in Mandarin, "Nǐ shībàile." (You failed). He then pushes me back onto the stage. I stumble backward and land on my butt.

I failed what?

I look back down the stairs, but the man is gone. Leo and the officers didn't notice.

The crowd's cheers revive as they spot me again on the stage, most likely assuming it's an encore. Seeing this, I stand and wave to the crowd and smile, keeping my lips sealed. I don't want that note slipping out. As I'm about to head back down the staircase, some of the high grass moves in the distance.

My eyes are playing tricks on me. You need sleep, Jimmy. Go deal with this Paradise City obstacle, then rest.

But as I look out again, grass, much closer to the crowd, ruffles violently. Hard thumping music emerges as a vehicle approaches. *No. It can't be.* I spit out the note from my mouth and read the perfectly written notecard, "九点见我们。丹佛."

See you at 9. Denver.

No.

Bursting out of the high grass come the Liberators. The extremist Communist terrorists run over a group of people in their rusted garbage truck. With their loud bass-heavy music blasting, the coked-out radicals jump from their truck and fire into the crowd with their Russian-made weapons.

Taking a step back, I watch as the terrorists shred the crowd. The majority of the armed crowd pulls out their guns. Confused as to who the enemy is, as the Liberators are dressed in similar attire as those in the crowd, some of the audience mistakenly shoot each other. The scene quickly turns into a blood bath. The mud becomes even slicker as it began to soak in the blood.

What have I done?

"Mr. President!" Leo screams and pulls me out of my trance, "C'mon, sir. We have to go! Now!" Leo grabs my slack body and drags me into my car. He opens the door of the black Cadillac SUV and pulls me into the back seat. "Drive!" he yells at the officer. The car starts, and we're gone.

I try to turn around to see the scene, but Leo grabs my shoulder.

"It's better not to look, sir. It makes keeping your character easier."

Was that mockery?

"Yeah," I say half-heartedly, "I guess it does."

With Leo's hand on my shoulder, we speed off into the night, trying to get to one of the last remaining major cities in the United States before nine. The road crumbles as the heavy Cadillac rolls over it. The surrounding neighborhood looks like a horror movie. The freshly bombed concrete crunches under the twenty-six-inch rims. The crater from a defective American bomb lies next to the road.

More gunshots behind me.

They did not earn this. They did not earn me. Instead, they're stuck with a President who is too scared to directly tell them we've lost this war. And now, I have to negotiate with people who want nothing more than to eliminate us from history to allow us to survive.

The surrounding neighborhood units are crumbling or already eliminated from the recent carpet bombing. A couple of small fires still burn along the cracked road.

What have I done?

CHAPTER 1

I HATE TALK SHOW DAY

LEVI O'SCANDRICK
DECEMBER 22, 2064

Bah! Bah! Bah!

The shades open, the lights blind me.

"Oh, Jesus!" Without opening my dry eyes, I smack my nightstand, trying to find my clock to turn off the screeching alarm. Instead, I hit a ceramic object. It cracks on the tile floor.

I jump out of bed and immediately search for the seashell lamp Kaiya made me for our thirteenth anniversary. The cold brown tile designed to look like a wood floor sends a shiver up my body. Black spots blur my vision. Lightheaded, my head spins like I'm on a merry-go-round riding a horse who had four-too-many shots of tequila. Snot drips down my pasty white nose. Sore throat. A ton of bricks on my chest. After a moment, the spins go away.

Please don't be broken, please don't be broken …

I examine the thin blue ceramic lamp. The six sporadically placed shells are still on the base. The white lampshade is crooked but not broken.

"Oh, thank God." My voice is hoarse. I choke on phlegm as I finish my exasperation.

Should I go spit? No, finish fixing the mess you made, then spit.

Bah! Bah! Bah!

I swallow and place the lamp back on the dark wooden nightstand next to a picture of Jackson dressed as a cowboy for Halloween. I smack the alarm clock next to it, and the horrible screech goes away. I scrape the rheum from my sandpapered eyes.

I've got to find a new sound for the alarm. This one jolts me too much.

My phone vibrates on the nightstand. On the screen is a picture of Kaiya kissing Jackson on the cheek when he was a baby. The caller ID reads "Kaiya Wandamaker (O'Scandrick)." Even better, now she's going to say, "I told you, you'd get sick. You shouldn't have swum in the community pools because they're disgusting, Levi."

I clear my throat and try to mask my obvious sickness, and say, "Yellow."

Music plays in the background of her call. Jackson yells something to his mom.

"Hey! Look who's finally awake. Did you get your beauty rest?" Kaiya's joy-filled voice is peppy like normal. But since my head decided to hurt today, it pierces my ear like she's stabbing me with a skewer.

"Yup."

I comb my thick brown hair to the side with my hand to tame it. I'm in my boxers, lean against the wall, and I study myself in the mirror. My hair looks electrocuted, but only half sticks out. My narrow jaw develops a five o'clock shadow, so I've got to shave. My slender build is more cut because of the lighting, not the workouts. My eyes seem sunken in because of the black rings, my nose dripping with snot.

Yeah, I definitely look presentable, but I've recovered from worse. "Ah, that's good to hear. What time is the monorail supposed to come in again?" she asks. Barely audible, I can make out Jackson saying something about a video game.

"Um, I think it's at noon. What's he saying?"

"No, sweetie," she says back in her *I knew you'd mess up* voice, "it's at 11:47."

"Yeah, but there's also the bullet at noon."

I yawn and stretch out my arms. Kaiya sighs disappointingly. Did she really expect anything else? "Check the schedule. The noon departure's been canceled. We talked about this last night." I take the phone off my ear and put her on speaker, with Jackson complaining to his mom. "What's he going on about?"

"Nothing, he just wants to play hide and seek in the middle of Norman's."

I give up on my hair, which has now devolved into a puffy ball. I scroll to the schedule for Friday, and sure enough ... "Ah shit," I say, disappointed, anticipating another sassy remark from my wife.

She pauses. I imagine her blue eyes twinkling as a smile runs across her thin, white face. "What would you do without me?" Kaiya says, smug. *Called it.*

"Be happy?" I joke. We both giggle lightly at that comment. Any other person would be offended. She's the best.

"Well, try to make sure you look presentable tonight. I hear Joe might pull a fast one and bring you on as a guest," she says mid-laugh.

What! She was serious about going to the show? Okay. Stay calm. Remember: yelling doesn't work. Be rational.

"Uh, no. I think I would rather die," I try to say lightheartedly, but it comes out more aggressive than I would have wished. "I mean, you know how much I dislike talk shows. Nothing good ever occurs on talk show day! It's like they intentionally ruin your morning just so they have an angered guest that would fall easily for drama triggers."

Kaiya, definitely expecting my response, gives her counterargument. "Levi, that was *one* time. And think of all the help it would give JJ and Aisling. I mean, it's their first time, and you've been on so many—"

"And I hated every second of it!" I respond hastily. *Remember no yelling? Do that.* "Plus," I continue, restraining my anger, "what happened to a stroll through The Dome tonight? I was really looking forward to that."

"We can do that any other day, Levi. They really need your help. Aisling even said so—"

"Aisling would never. I remember her explicitly telling me she didn't need my help."

"Yes, but she is also extremely stubborn and—"

"Which is exactly why I shouldn't interfere. You remember what happened on Christmas. She lost her mind when I tried to make a drink that wasn't on her preset menu."

"Levi, you can overcome your fear for one night, right? People won't bug you too much today when you're with Jackson."

"Jackson's going? He can't be there. It's … uh, inappropriate."

A long pause ensues as Kaiya's anger with my stubbornness peaks. She's mad, but she's not her normal arguing self. Something's off.

"I didn't want to pull this card—" she says.

Oh no.

"but …"

Please don't.

"I already told Aisling you would."

And there it is. Nail in the coffin.

"What? Why would you do that?"

"Because I knew you'd say no, and Aisling already asked me."

"Will I be on there with them?"

"Well, yeah, obviously. They said they'll pull you from the audience and onto the show, so they won't psych you out like last time."

"Fine, I'll consider it. But they owe me."

She's too persistent. She's got something planned.

"Yay!" she chirps, as if winning the lottery, "I'll let them know. Now go make yourself look good. What time does the 11:47 monorail get in?"

I reopen the app and look at the schedule. "It says 4:33, but knowing this system, it's probably around 5."

"Okay, well, you better hurry. It's already 11:36." The red digital numbers on the clock on my dresser display 11:36 a.m. I turn back to the mirror and reevaluate my disgruntled appearance. *How come time flies so fast when you just wake up?* "Um, honey … I got to go."

"Ha! Called it," she says, then laughs her childish squeal. Then, further away from the phone, "Daddy messed up again."

Over the speaker, much clearer this time, Jackson gleefully yells, "Ha ha, Daddy's an idiot!"

Ha ha, leverage!

"Wha—what are you teaching him that for?"

"I didn't teach him that! He's been saying that all day after hearing you say it, and much worse, on your phone calls yesterday." *Fell for the trap again.* You would think I would have learned by now, but I guess I'm just that gullible.

"You should also take a decongestant. Jackson says you sound like a frog," she teases.

"Oh, did he now?" I say as a smirk crawls onto my face. The clock reads 11:38. "Crap, I have to go. Love you, bye," I say quickly as I put on a plain navy-blue button-down.

"Love you, bye," she responds and hangs up.

I toss the phone onto my bed. It takes a bad roll off the white sheets and hits the cedar tile floor. From a distance, there are no major cracks. Lucky this time.

I hold up the clothing options in the mirror. I barely have an opportunity to make myself presentable. So, blue shirt, gray pants, and gray sport coat. Blue shoes? No, black or …

A loud explosion shakes my three three-story home. I hit the deck, expecting the worst. Crawling over to the bedroom window on the third floor, I try to look outside, but another crash sends me away. They've finally come.

At least my final words were, "I love you."

But Jackson … no, I've got to make it through this.

Crawling on the cold tile floor, I climb over the two aluminum racks of shoes and reach the safe hidden in the back of my closet. Typing in the code, the three-foot silver cube opens, revealing my bull-barreled .44. Outside, military officers scream orders at their robotic soldiers. My shaking hand loads the pistol.

The heavy boom of footsteps stepping in unison echoes across the Little Village. There must be at least fifty. *Stop. Breathe. Think.* The only entrances they have are through the bottom story window and the doors. Did I forget to lock the doors? Stone is crushed outside. *What the hell's that?*

A couple of seconds pass in silence before the first story door bursts open. Officers storm through my home. Their footprints shake the failing structure. More stone crushed on the outside.

I probably have twelve seconds before they reach the third story and find my room, so I crawl over to my door, gun in hand. I close the door silently. As the heavy footsteps run up the stairs, the stone-crushing intensifies. A pattern emerges. In unison, a four-step pattern. They're scaling the walls.

Officers yelling generic orders become clearer as the footsteps cease. Their shadows are visible under my door. They pound, trying to break down the reinforced steel inside the white wooden door. The officers scaling the walls closing in are about to reach my window.

This is it. This is how I die.

I can't believe it. I had finally found the one thing that made me sane, but, like the rest of my life, once accomplished, the pendulum swings back. At least it's poetic, I guess. But Jackson and Kaiya have to make it without me. If these officers don't immediately kill me, maybe I can plead a trial. I'll lose, no doubt, but hopefully, I can pull enough heartstrings to guarantee Kaiya and Jackson's safety. It doesn't matter how they remember me, just that they're safe.

As the officers break the glass, I close my eyes and raise my arms in surrender, but before they kill me, the doorbell rings. It rings again. Then again. I open my eyes slowly.

There are no officers in my room. It's the exact same as I'd left it: the cedar wood floor tiles still on the floor, my white queen-sized bed unmade, my closet and bathroom door open.

My doorbell stops ringing. Something hits my window with a sharp bang. My phone buzzes on the floor. I crawl to the other side of the room. What's happening? Where'd the bots go? My breathing, sporadic and heavy, becomes a chore.

I need to calm down. Another object hits my window again with a sharp ping. I freeze. The bots, are they back?

No. Get out of your own head.

I take a deep breath and think of Kaiya. Her face appears. We are on our first date. Eating at Bob's Loving Sandwiches at my request. I don't know at the time that she's a vegetarian, so when she orders the twenty-two (a ham sandwich with a lot of veggie toppings) without the ham, I'm confused. The face I see right now is her reaction to me scrambling and apologizing to her for not knowing that. She smiles, showing off her pretty white teeth. Her nose crinkles up as she laughs.

She had pulled her loose, baggy blue-top back above her shoulder and said, "It's fine. Don't feel bad. You'd be surprised how many times this happens."

With that scene in my head, my breathing returns to normal.

My hand releases its relentless grip on my gun.

I shouldn't worry. I have a beautiful, now pregnant wife and a son, who both love me, waiting to meet me at *The Late Show*. I am going to see my best friend JJ and his wife Aisling achieve an accomplishment that no one has dared to even think about, besides me, of course.

Smile. Everything is going to be all right.

The doorbell rings again, taking me out of my fantasy.

My phone vibrates, my jackass neighbor Robert McKinley calling me. He throws another pebble from my front porch to my third-story window. I get up off the floor and place the gun on my bed. Out the window, McKinley's gold Chevy Camaro is crushed under a large, black, raised pickup truck.

Being the middle house on the cul-de-sac round means I can see everything. A couple of neighbors are outside taking pictures and videos of the crash. A teenage girl yells out, "I got it recorded right here!" as if it's a triumph.

Another teenager, most likely the one whose car is on top of McKinley's pimp mobile, is sitting on the curb next to the two vehicles on McKinley's front lawn. He is a young Asian man with a high black Mohawk, maroon shirt, and tight charcoal jeans.

Since when is that back in style?

"Hey!" an old, raspy, muffled voice yells at me from far away, "Answer your phone!" McKinley's at my front door. Big car crash, yelling, the banging on the window. *Well, that explains a lot. What an ass.*

I grab my phone and reenter my closet, noticing that this panic attack took away four minutes of my life. Just throw on the blue and gray basic stuff and explain the hair as "intentionally sloppy, a new look I'm trying out ... What do you think?"

I answer the phone, "I'm not going to help you, Bob," I say hastily.

"Look out your window, you supposed genius! This fucking airhead just totaled my car!" McKinley's voice is raspy due to the heavy smoking. Too bad it didn't stop him from being loud or just killed him.

"And you should be thanking him," I say as I put on my silk navy shirt. "You looked like the captain of douche university in that thing."

"What did you say to me, yuh bastard? I swear to God ..." I look at the clock. 11:41. I don't have time for this. Putting my pants on, I say, "Have you paid me for the last repair?" Bob stammers and says, "Well, no. I told you I can't till they lower the tax again."

Socks? Sure.

"Then we have nothing else to talk about."

"Levi! You're the only mechanic here, so that's the only reason why I'm even asking you."

"Wrong again, Bob. Just because I fixed your car once doesn't mean—"

"Oh, you know what I mean," Bob interrupts. "Come down here and—"

"Sorry, Bob," I say, choking on mucus.

Decongestant.

I open the medicine cabinet and grab a pill, and finish the conversation with, "I've got a monorail to catch." I hang up the phone with Bob yelling through it.

I step out of the bathroom, look at myself in the mirror on my closet door.

Yup, that's definitely passable.

I grab the keys to my pickup, Baby Bertha, and catch a glimpse of the .44 on my bed. I grab the gun, quickly unload it, and put it back in the safe. I don't need it. I can't keep letting my paranoia win. The clock reads 11:44. I take a deep breath, exit my room, and jog down the stairs.

"I hate talk show day," I say with disdain.

CHAPTER 2

WELCOME TO PARADISE

LEVI O'SCRANDRICK
DECEMBER 22, 2064

As I jog out to Baby Bertha, three houses down, McKinley yells at the goth kid. His house looks like crap, aside from the now dented gold Chevy Camaro and new rubble on his green artificial lawn. His Spanish-style home is the same build as the rest that line the lone street in Little Village 18, only his is filthy. With a chipped paint job, his house looks like the perfect setting for a horror show.

"Imma sue your ass for wrecking my baby," yells McKinley at the kid.

I get into Baby Bertha, turn on the battery, and drive off, hoping McKinley doesn't see me. Actually, I can have a little fun with it. Am I a jerk for mocking a senile old man? Yes. Do I care? No. As I drive past him, I roll down my window and, mimicking his husky New York accent, yell at him, "Just remember, Bob, he did you a favor, yuh fat bastard."

"Aye, fuck you, Levi! You look like a bitch in a teal pickup truck! Only bitches get those! Hey, don't you drive away from me, yuh bastard!"

I laugh as I speed down the road. It's just too easy with this guy. I look out the rearview window as I turn on AutoDrive. The kid seems ... angry. As if insulting McKinley hurt his feelings. It's just my paranoia. One episode's enough for a day.

I continue to drive down the single road. Our twenty-five-foot-high electrified perimeter fence lines the street like a cage for zoo animals. All life in this Little Village is in those homes. The rest of the trip is barren. The clock reads 11:45 a.m. Speeding won't get me there much faster. I turn on our one radio station, 99.7 New York's Finest. The president is speaking. Really? He is seriously on the radio spreading more of his filth and crazy propaganda? He has sold us out. What more does he want?

He begins in his deep, grumbly New York accent, "Our nation is facing the largest catastrophe it has ever seen. There are children walking naked in the streets and their mothers unable to provide for them. Crime rules our once beautiful, elegant, and thriving cities, and law and order are gone. We need to take back what is ours. This world, this America, we live in is not the one I want nor what anyone should want."

"Look, after we lost the war, things changed. *People* changed. We got desperate and paranoid. We let *them*, those pathetic Russian and Chinese scum, win. Sure, they bombed our homes, slaughtered our soldiers, and ruined our nation, but they can't take away our character. That is only something we can hand to them, and ... we're doing it."

Yeah, they used our bombs. You surrendered everything to them. I know he is the one who sold us out. He gave them our codes and let them dismantle our nuclear arsenal, allowing them to eliminate us with ease. All for what? Money? Despicable. That's blood on your hands, Jimmy.

"How many of you selflessly help one another? How many of you would stop the shooting of a stranger because it's the right thing to do? We need people like this in our great nation if we want to recover from what they did to us."

New low now by blaming us for his failures. What? We're not allowed to make our own choices anymore?

"So, my message to you, my fellow Americans, is not to give in to the despair this apocalypse brought to us. If you do so, you are only letting the Russians and Chinese win. And that is something I will never want to say again. Thank you for your time. Your President, Saint Jimmy."

A stupid song that has no meaning proceeds to play.

"Ha!" I yell to myself. "He really calls himself St. Jimmy now? Great, what's next? He's going to start calling himself God, and we're going to kill ourselves over him? He is the problem with America, not us! He spits these beautiful speeches that just divide us. It's his way or the highway? Give me a break. He's the one who sold us to the Russians and Chinese. Any person who says that Russia and China, two evil communist countries, are our allies does not deserve to be president. He is the problem with our country. Not me!"

A brunette woman with big sunglasses and a black leopard print scarf around her head stares at me from the next lane over. She snickers.

"Oh, it's not like you've never yelled at yourself alone in your car before!" I scream.

She laughs and steps on the gas of her little red sports car, passing me.

Dumb broad.

"Your car makes no sense for the world we live in! You're wasting your life, and … she can't hear me."

Embarrassed and pissed off at myself and the corruption in our government, I slam off the radio. I drive the rest of the way in silence, taking in the hideous outside. Today is looking pretty bad compared to others, which is saying something. Rain is starting to fall despite minimal cloud coverage. The rain is dark and thick, almost like a dark gray mud. The electrified black chain-link dome that surrounds us sparkles as it zaps the rain off its electric fencing.

I arrive at the monorail station and park my car in one of the twelve spots outside. *Remember not to look left.* The gray stone station looks like an ancient Greek temple, with concrete (instead of marble) pillars and a pyramid roof. The stone pillars that barely hold the old station together are chipped and cracked from a lack of maintenance. The station opens to the parking lot with no walls or doors, so all the dirt and dust from the outside slides in.

I walk past the pillars and onto the cold gray concrete floor. One lone bench sits in the middle of the platform facing the tracks. As I approach the seat, I turn to the ticket dispenser. It's not on. The little screen in the center of the chest-high red machine is cracked. The wall of the dreadful ticket booth next to the dispenser is missing the monitor that states the events for the week. A clean box stains the wall where the monitor used to be.

Great, now I have to talk to the stupid machine.

I approach the ugly concrete ticket booth. It protrudes out of the wall for about four feet. Under the clean box, the side of the booth has an engraving of the American flag being raised at Iwo Jima.

Just yell skip intro this time. If I keep yelling, it should shut up. The Replacement in the dimly lit ticket booth is Latina, with black hair, brown eyes, and tan skin. It has cat eye reading glasses on and a black and white polka dot dress.

"Skip intro!" I yell.

"Hello," it responds in a gentle female voice. It continues and smiles, saying, "My name is Barbara …"

"Skip intro!"

"… and I am, despite my *beautiful* appearance …"

"Skip intro!"

"—not a human being. I am a synthetically created human created for the purpose of doing menial labor …"

"Skip the damn intro!"

Its smile fades, and she returns to her generic, emotionless face, "I'm sorry to have angered you. Would you like to file a complaint?"

"No! Just get me a zone one ticket."

"Processing …" It pauses and prints a zone one ticket from her wrist. The ticket lands in her hand. It reaches out of the booth and hands it to me. *I wonder which number she, damn, it, is.* The number 1752 is tattooed on her wrist.

Ha! 1,752 attempts, and this is the best they can do?

I laugh and walk away. My chuckle fades at the end of the tracks. Past the pillars is the entrance, rather a "one-way exit" into Nowhere. The seventy-foot, electrified gate sits only a couple of meters from the edge of the station. Two snipers sit comfortably in their nests inside the gate, waiting to shoot anyone who crosses their self-decided comfort zone. Four different guards lean against the pillars with their flamethrowers and pistols, waiting to clean up those who willingly toss themselves onto the fence, hoping death will be better than their life. *Disgraceful. The gate's all just a show.*

They twist it into yet another tool used for oppression. Bile rises in my throat.

Control yourself. Take a deep breath and move on.

My eyes disobey my thoughts. The vast emptiness beyond the black gate into Nowhere always amazes me in some horrifying way. The ground is gray and dusty, almost like a salt flat. With each step of a guard's boot, a pile of dust plumes knee-high into the toxic air.

How can anyone survive out there? The soil is useless, and the water is most likely poison, so how can anyone make it?

Today, three of the Others sit on the opposite side of the fence, spaced twenty meters from the entrance into the Little Village. They are wrapped in gray and green stained puffy jackets, scarves, and multiple layers of blankets. They stare at me.

A mother with brown hair, pale skin, and blank brown eyes is lying with her two children. The mother is motionless on the ground, her brown eyes staring blankly into the station. She most likely died of starvation, given the lack of wounds on her body. Her infant lies next to her screaming, wrapped in a dark green shirt. The older child, a young blond girl, is sobbing, shaking her mother as if trying to wake her from her sleep.

The daughter notices my gaze. Her blue eyes and pale face cut into my heart. I want to help, but I know I can't. If I take one step toward them, I know I'll have an even worse fate than they do. I turn my back to the family and sit on the sole bench in the station. The infant's screams continue to plague me. I restrain tears from flooding my eyes as the 11:47 a.m. monorail pulls into the station from the right. A couple of black burn marks scar the top of the white monorail, most likely given by another Molotov cocktail attack by the Others.

As if on cue to my arrival, the hum of trucks approach from Nowhere. One of them carries two gatekeepers who have flamethrowers and a pistol strapped to their side. They each wear thick, black, fire-retardant suits and a bulletproof black helmet. On their chests are the yellow letters P.C.N.Y. (Paradise City: New York).

The other is a smaller van that has a cage in it. A woman wearing a white lab coat, a gas mask, and black boots steps out and walks toward the infant. My heart sinks as I helplessly watch. The daughter screams and frantically shakes her mother.

The gatekeepers approach the kids. The woman tries to grab the baby, but the daughter fights her for control. A guard kicks her in the head with his massive boot. She falls flat. I can barely see if she's moving because of the thick dust cloud forming around the skirmish. The woman in the lab coat proceeds to grab the infant and run into the smaller van, which then drives away.

I can do something.

The broad from the red sports car brushes past me with her headphones on, intently focused on her phone, oblivious to the situation. As she enters, I look at the now open door of the monorail.

No, I can't.

If I go out there, I'm dead. The result will be the same, except Jackson will have no father. I can't do anything. My nose tingles, and my eyes burn as tears fill them. I can't watch this. I scan my ticket and follow the lady onto the monorail, letting the doors seal shut behind me. Taking my seat, I turn away from the chaos. The infant's screams continue to haunt me. I think of the mother, the daughter, and the baby.

I couldn't have done anything. Right?

The woman in the stupid red sports car sits across from me. She now has her phone projected newspaper out. My face on the cover. She stares at me with disgust, realizing who I am. I cover my face with my hands. Typical, but it's the deal.

Bang! Bang!

I close my eyes. Shiver. The high-pitched scream of the daughter. The deafening shots of pistols being fired. Followed by the painful sound of silence. The infant is gone, to be brainwashed and trained as an expendable soldier for Marshall. The mother and daughter, just another Other burnt to ash. Never even known to exist.

My breathing is sporadic, my heart pounding through my chest. My head was heavy and overfilled, like a bowling ball. My body tingles with pins and needles.

No. Stop. Breathe. Calm Down.

Taking a deep breath, I say out loud, "Don't worry. I have a beautiful, now pregnant wife Kaiya and my son Jackson, who both love me, waiting to meet me at *The Late Show*. I am going to see my best friend JJ and his wife Aisling present their hard work for our world to enjoy. Smile. Everything is going to be all right."

Taking another deep breath, I see Kaiya and Jackson on the red and yellow swing in our backyard. Jackson tries to go higher than his mom, but the restraints I put into the swing to prevent it from flipping won't allow him. "Why can't I go any higher," Jackson asks as he swings his legs harder. Kaiya just laughs, avoiding giving away our secret. Relaxed, I smile, simply removing myself from one reality and forcing myself into another where everything will always be all right.

CHAPTER 3

NO NAMES

ALI SCHOLTZ
DECEMBER 22, 2064

"And that's when I realized how we really messed this whole thing up," Charlie says in his deep, barreling voice, chuckling. Through his reflection in the window, he glares at me.

Outside, the purple sunrise lights up the sky. The surrounding trading shops and stores built beautifully out of sheet metal and concrete blocks create shadows across the cracked five-lane highway. Hundreds of people clump together in the wide street. Their breaths form a cloud around them. They bump into each other like the ants do when they climb the legs of our table.

My tiny notebook, pen, and sticks of gum I keep in my pocket press against my gray jeans. I roll up the white sleeves of the button-down, looking more cut. My arms got a little more definition in them now.

"Ali, are you even listening to me?" Charlie questions angrily.

Oh dammit! I did it again.

I turn around, bracing for a well-deserved tell-off. The tiny apartment we're in is in great shape compared to the other holdout I was in before. This one has a wooden floor that has a couple of air bubbles in it. The yellow walls are only mildly chipped, which is a big plus. Most of the yellow cabinets are still on their hinges, a sink, but no water, and, most importantly, a working fridge!

I've got to make this run the best one of my life. I need to have this place! I don't have to walk sixteen miles to get water anymore! I can just go downstairs.

Charlie sits in the only chair next to the circular wooden dinner table. His tan face just shows pure disappointment. His black hair is spiked up high. He wears a white t-shirt, a black bomber, black joggers, and running shoes.

"I'm sorry, Charlie. I was just curious. How did they build the shops so well? I mean, they look … fantastic. Like the real buildings in those movies you showed me," I say, lightly trying to show him I wasn't just blankly looking at a window just to blankly look out a window. There was a purpose!

Charlie's face isn't giving me any hints. If he's mad, I can't tell. He rolls his eyes and says, *not* angrily, "Did you even hear a word I said?"

"Yes. I mean, of course," I stutter, trying to keep my composure. "Your sister tried sneaking out of the house and …" I can't lie to him. He's too damn smart for that.

Just tell him the truth.

"Yeah, that's basically it," Charlie interrupts before I can give my admission. He gives me a look that says, "Pay attention this time." Then continues, "She has this crush on this guy, um, we'll call him Bruce. So Bruce invited her out, right. Cuz he's been tryna get with her for like an entire year," he says and, and chuckles, showing off his white teeth. "Oh my

God, the things he did. Anyway, our parents had no interest in my sister dating some bum like him. So, they told her she couldn't go out with him. And she was not having it! I mean, I still remember the yelling match her and my mom had."

He switches his accent to one I don't know. It sounds kinda nasally, "'Why you going out dressed like a hoe! I didn't raise you like that!'" He then switches to higher-pitched squeaky voice, "'Mom! You can't tell me what to wear! I'm going out like this, and that's it!'" He laughs after he finished the sentence.

Is there something I'm missing here? Why is this funny? I don't understand. Does this have to do with my run? Wait, what was the route for the traps again? Turn one leads to a gun, but turn right and ...

He continues after wiping a tear from his eye, "And then there was me, doing my thing. But I had to sneak out too cuz our mom," he says and whistles. His smile was full of joy. "Boy, you think sneaking into Paradise Cities is hard? Try sneaking out of my house. Shit was like those internment camps we had all those years back. You know it's funny how fast and easy things fall apart. It only takes one dumbass to bring down a building. But it takes a genius to put it back together."

Ugh, what's his jingle? 'Turn one leads to a gun, turn right, and you'll be all right.' Okay, then it goes, 'Go straight to the count of thirty-two or else get skewered by three dudes. Pause and wait to the count of eight, or else turn to a slab of bait. Dodge the ...' Crap, what's the dodge one? 'Dodge the ...'

Charlie looks me in the eye. His excitement disappears, and his smile turns into his normal firm and stoic face. He's angry like I did something wrong. He calls me out, saying, "Man, what is with you and that window? I'm putting my past in front of you, and you ignore it!" He's obviously mad at me for not listening, but I'm just too stressed! What does he expect me to do, sit and listen to funny stories I don't understand?

Tell him the truth. Redeem yourself.

"I'm sorry, Charlie," I say tentatively, "I'm just really nervous. Can we go over the rules and the jingle again? I'm not sure I've got it." Charlie sits on the chair. I can't figure out if he's mad or not, and he says, "Hey, you don't need to. It's bad luck to study on the day of the test. Don't you know that?"

Well, I never graduated eighth grade, but you don't need to know about that.

Out of nowhere, a timer goes off. Charlie reaches into his pocket and pulls out the tiny orange timer. He puts it onto the wooden table. "Sit," he says firmly to me as he walks to the closest yellow wall.

Okay. Take a deep breath. Rule one: No names because it's harder to let the people go after we cross, and names can make me do "stupid ass decisions," like the last time. Rule two: ...

Charlie puts his hand on the wall. Two quick beeps come and go, then a slot on the wall opens. Charlie grabs my backpack from the hole. *Wow. That's impressive. We need these in all the safehouses.*

Charlie puts the bulletproof, black camo backpack on the wooden table. It lands with a thud. He then opens the two grenade tubes on either side of the backpack to see if they're full. There are five hurt grenades on the left and five concussions on the right. He closes the tubes and then opens the backpack itself. Charlie pulls out the supplies: a six-inch knife, a Glock 19 with a silencer, two rounds of bullets, two rounds of tranquilizer darts, and …

Yes! Two of my favorite black smoke grenades. I love when the Rat Hunters or soldiers think its toxic and run away. I don't know why, but watching them flee always cheers me up. "Everything good?" Charlie asks as he looks at his timer. "Yes. Everything's perfect," I respond anxiously, "But Charlie, can we please just go over the rules one more time? I know, I know, 'bad luck,' and all, but I really need to do this. It'll help put my mind straight."

Charlie sighs and reluctantly says, "Fine. Rule one?"

"No names because it's harder to let the people go after we cross, and names can make me do 'stupid ass decisions,' like the last time because I have too big a heart."

"Rule two?"

"My life is more valuable than theirs, but that shouldn't stop me from trying to save their lives. So, stay alive, and keep them alive. But stay alive more. Rule three ..."

"Rule three?" Charlie questions.

Did he forget rule three?

"Rule three: No killing because ..."

"Ali," Charlie interrupts. He collects himself and says, "I'm sorry to tell you this again, but you may have to kill on this particular run. I know it's not what you want or what I've shown you, but you're an adult now. You are a runner. A coyote. Your goal is ..."

"To successfully transfer the people who deserve a better life into the cities that were taken from them. Yeah, I know, Charlie."

"And if that means you have to shoot someone ... I'm sorry, Ali, I know that's not up your alley, but sometimes ... sometimes success means doing something you don't want to do for the betterment of others. Now is killing wrong? Yes, absolutely, but these people deserve ... um," Charlie stops and locks eyes with me. His eyes scrunch together like they do when he thinks too hard.

Am I making a face?

He continues, "The people we are saving, Ali. They deserve a better life than the one that's been dealt to them. Through no fault of their own, they've been cast out by the greedy monsters in the Paradise Cities and left out here. Do you know what they call this place, Ali?"

"The Funstein Trading Mile?"

"No! Stop being so literal. Ali, they call this place, where we live, our home, Nowhere. They don't even have the decency to call us a part of their country! We live in a separate place from them, and all they want is for us to drop dead. Now you don't want that Ali, do you?"

"No! Of course not."

"Then don't feel so bad about it." He hands me our standard Glock 19. The cold metal of the gun feels heavy in my scruffy hands.

Wait, is this some sort of test? I think it is. If I take the gun, I'm not good enough to be a coyote. But what if the test is for me to take the gun and not use it? Oh, that's a good one. And all the people in the stories Charlie tells us don't kill. So I don't have to either.

The stopwatch on the table beeps loudly. I look up at Charlie, who already has my backpack in his hand. I grab the stopwatch and knife from the table and dip.

"Okay, Ali. I believe in you. All right? You've … you've got this," Charlie says encouragingly as he walks me out the door. I stumble out into the dark hallway. The door closes with a big thud.

CHAPTER 4

NO TALKING

ALI SCHOLTZ
DECEMBER 22, 2064

I stand in the dark hallway of the second floor of the store. *Okay, Ali. You've got this. Even Charlie said it. You've got this. Just walk in that door, jump buildings, then take these people to Paradise. Easy ... Easy. Easy. Easy. Totally easy.* I breathe deeply and open the green door of the entry room. This hideout is a lot uglier than the one I was in before. Instead of it being clean and pretty, the gray walls are molded, the floor is concrete, and there's only a metal folding chair in the room. *Wow, I get spoiled for one minute, and now this isn't good enough for me? Relax, me. I'm not rich enough to complain.*

I enter the room and walk immediately to the back wall. I take off the backpack and open it. I grab both smoke grenades and the knife and strap them to my belt loops. I then look at the Glock. *He said it's okay to kill. He told me that it may come to that. But none of the heroes have done it, so why should I? Ugh, fine, just in case.* I stash the Glock in the back of my pants, so I'm not tempted to use it.

After I complete my setup, I stare blankly at the concrete wall. *What did he say about the door? Oh yeah, start left and go right. Knock at shoulder level till I hear the hollowness? Hollow sound?* I walk over to the left side of the wall and knock. *Nope.* I take one step right after each knock and listen to the sound. Finally, after like five steps, I find the door. *Okay, this is it. Now time to kick it down.* I take five steps back. *Just run and kick, run and kick, run and kick. Easy.* I run and front kick the wall but miss and kick the concrete. "Ow! Son of a bitch!" My leg feels like, well, like I just kicked a wall of concrete.

"What does 'hollow' even mean, anyway? All I know is that it means the wall would break instead of my leg!"

I limp over to a random spot further down the wall and kick it in frustration. Instead of bouncing off like it should have, cracks from where my foot was. *Luck benefits the bold! Ha ha!* I take five paces back and brace for my kick. *Okay, left leg this time.* Running over, I kick through the wall. Luckily for me, the entire wall collapses around me, making sure everyone around me knows I'm here. Looking down from the second story, I see the remains. It landed down in between me and the next building in a big pile. *Huh, they're gonna be pissed.*

"Hey, will you shut up!" a gravelly voice screams. "He's going to be on the second floor in like one minute, so hurry your ass up and get there!"

I look closer and recognize three people, tatted up like crazy. One dude's gotta big beard and a bunch of tattoos on his neck and face. The other one's taller than the other but really skinny. The third guy disappears before I can get a good look. The two here wear all black and are strapped with AK-47 rifles. Their hats have camouflaged American flags on the front. Typical Rat Hunters.

Who tipped these guys off? Rat Hunters aren't smart enough to do this on their own. Wrights definitely bought off a couple of sellers here.

"Shit!" I yell louder than I wanted. The two Rat Hunters whip their heads around and snarl. "Double shit," I whimper.

The hunters start shooting. I flop down on the ground tryna to avoid the gunfire. Waiting for these guys to reload, I prep my leg for the jump. Above me, a pipe extends to the next home where my package is. *Great. I can just use that, swing over. Easy. So easy.* I push back on my leg, getting used to the pain.

Why am I such a dumbass? I really gotta start learning some more words.

The bullets stop. Jumping, pain shoots through my leg, but I am able to grab the pipe. I climb as fast as I can to get to the next home and shatter the window. Stumbling through, I try to run. My leg's on fire. My arm cut from the glass. Blood stains my sleeve.

I take a deep breath. Icy sheet metal covers the room. The cold outdoor air and the metal make a typical New York ... or now I guess Nowhere refrigerator. A couple of boxes of food are in the corner.

Where the hell are these people? We told them the second floor.

Blood is starting to drip onto the floor from my arm. I cover the cut up with my hand.

Before I even look around the room, two grappling hooks clank to the second-story ceiling. The wire struggles to pull up the Rat Hunters.

Shit. That's new.

Gripping my arm, I open the door of the fridge and run. *Where the hell are these people?*

I open the door of the room across the hall. There are two beds, a couple of toys, and an empty fishbowl, but no people. I close the door and run down a wooden staircase, which creaks under each step.

As I exit the staircase, there's whimpering. *Oh, there they are! They probably think I'm a robber or something.* I turn to find a ball-peen hammer approaching my face. Reacting probably more aggressively than I should, I grab the woman's arm and put my hand on her mouth to quiet her scream. Behind her is another woman with darker skin, long black hair, and a very surprised look on her face. A little boy and a little girl who look very similar hide next to her: milky skin, green eyes, dirty blond hair. The woman I am holding has a shaved head with a scar across the right side. Two wings and two antennas are drawn on the scar, making it look like a butterfly.

Taking my hand off the first woman's mouth, I point up to the ceiling. The two Rat Hunters land in the room and grunt as if the climb was just too much for them. The woman's green eyes widen even further.

Why is she still tweaking? I'm here to help her. Why does she ... oh yeah.

I show her the black box tattoo I have on my left wrist. She sees it and relaxes.

"Where that little fucker go?" yells one of the Rat Hunters in his gravelly voice.

The two women and kids look up, scared. The little girl steps up to the bald lady in front with her fists clenched. The little boy follows closely behind. *Ah, that's cute. They're gonna fight the Rat Hunters. Ah, these guys are just adorable.* The other woman with hair hands me an all-black card to show that they are my package.

"He's here. He's just hiding with his pests," says the other Rat Hunter in a smoother, calm voice.

Okay, so there are two upstairs. One ran around, probably to the front door, so that's a big no-no. Is there another exit?

Sunlight seeps through the cracks in the concrete and lights up the dust in the air. To our left is another white door, probably a closet, and past that is another room. The front door is right in front of me. Next to it, a broken mirror that fell on the floor. To the right, just a big wall.

Great, so the front door it is. One is better than two.

I tap the bald lady with the butterfly on her head. *Should I call her Butterfly? Butterfly Head?* I tap Butterfly on the shoulder and point to the front door. She looks at me, confused.

Was that not clear? I'm pretty sure pointing is a well-known, like, gesture for "go that way."

I point again at the door, and she shakes her head no.

What? Does she want to die?

I nod my head yes. She continues to shake her head. The other woman, with the long black hair, touches my shoulder. I turn around to her, and she points to the other room to my left.

Oh, so there is another exit.

I smile at her, tap my head to say, "good thinking," and slowly walk to the room. The family follows.

"Yeah, but where did he go?" the gravelly voice guy whispers loudly. He sounds a lot closer to us, then a loud smack.

"If I knew that, you dipshit, I wouldn't have said, 'he's hiding' the first time you asked! You see anything down there?"

"Nah, nothing yet," says another Rat Hunter in the room next to us.

Where the fuck did he come from? Dammit!

The Rat Hunter has his back turned to the mirror next to the front door, looking around what I think is the kitchen. *Okay, so black gas in the kitchen, concussion up the stairs, and bail through the front door. Simple.* I turn back toward the group, but they are heading back toward the closet door.

No! Why are they not following me? It's literally all they have to do. Butterfly gestures for me to go into the closet. *Oh, so now she knows what that means.* I shake my head and point to my grenade, make a throwing gesture, and then point to the front door. She points again to the closet and mouths, "Basement."

Ugh, they're going to get us killed in there.

The Rat Hunters' footsteps are getting closer, and the two from upstairs are getting closer. *This is what Rule two is for. I can escape and save myself. It's easy. Really easy.* There's hurt in the bald lady's eyes. I can't leave these people. I'm their last hope for getting the life taken from them. That's what Charlie said. So that means I've gotta be the good hero. I quietly move over to the basement. As I do, I grab a black smoke grenade from my belt and throw it up the stairs at the bedroom. It hits the ground, and the black smoke fills the air.

"Told you he's here. Masks on boys!" yells the gravelly-voiced guy.

As the smoke quickly fills the room, I set a timer on the two hurt grenades for fifteen seconds and the other for forty-five seconds. The other Rat Hunter that was in the kitchen emerges as I close the door behind the bald lady and me.

Ah, I don't even get to watch them run away from the smoke.

In the near pitch-black basement, the only light comes from under the door. I'm sitting on the second stair closest to the door. One of the kids whimpers behind me.

Please work. Please work.

"He's upstairs! In the bedroom!" yells the guy with a gravelly voice. Heavy footsteps start to run past us. However, before the third Rat Hunter runs up the stairs, he stops. I look down at my arm. Blood from the cut drips on the floor. Blood on the doorway too. The Rat Hunter's shadow blocks the light from coming through the bottom of the doorway. One of the kids behind me whimpers louder.

If I heard that from the stairs coming down here, they can too.

"He's not up here!" yells the guy with a gravelly voice. "You fucking idiot! You just gave away our position!" yells the other guy. The Rat Hunter in front of the door chuckles to himself.

Please, blow up. Please blow up.

The Rat Hunter takes a step back and cocks his gun. *If I use the gun, I can shoot first and kill him.* I reach for the gun in the back of my pants. Before I can grab it, the first hurt grenade explodes.

Now's our chance.

I open the door and grab Butterfly so that she can't say no. Opening the door, I run directly at the first Rat Hunter and bash him in the nose with the butt of the gun. I push Butterfly to the front door and then hit the Rat Hunter in the face again with the gun, knocking him out.

Rubble and debris cover the top floor from the gigantic hole in the ceiling. Black smoke lit up by the sun.

I stare at the gun in my hand.

I can't believe I almost used this. That would've been so bad. I would've been just like them. I can't let this happen again.

I throw the Glock up the stairs. It lands, and a shot fires. The Rat Hunters shoot at the sound.

I turn around and find the front door wide open and run. The family stands outside, staring at their home. They blend in with the massive crowd of people, who scatter from the explosion. The little boy's green eyes are teary and wide open.

Oh, he must be scared they're gonna come back out and chase us.

I kneel down to look the boy in the eyes. "Oh, I wouldn't worry about them, little guy," I try to say as sweetly as I can, "Rat Hunters, huh, so dumb. Am I right? They'll be stuck in there for hours until they figure out we left." As I say that, the other hurt grenade explodes. I turn around as the left wall of the house caves in. A large dust cloud forms around the house as it collapses. The Rat Hunters keep yelling at each other and fire into thin air.

Ha ha! That's what you get when you mess with Ali Scholtz!

I turn around with a smirk on my face, only for the entire family to stare at their house so sadly.

Oh yeah, empathy.

"Uh huh, shall we?" I ask playfully.

The family still stares at their home. The daughter clings to Butterfly, who is still holding her hammer. Lady Black Hair hugs the little boy.

Great start, Ali. Great start. Hey, why don't you just blow up the entire trading mile while you're at it!

"I'm sorry about your house, but think about it, you're getting a better one once we get to Paradise City: New York!" I say over-enthusiastically.

Lady Black Hair turns around and says kinda sassily, "Where now?"

"Glad you asked," I say happily, trying to lighten the family's spirits. "We are taking that," I point to the red four-seater dune buggy parked in the body shop across the store, "all the way to the entry point. We're one step closer to Paradise. Yay!"

The family walks to the dune buggy.

Jeez, try to at least act excited.

I push through the crowd of people and head to the dune buggy.

See, I was able to get the family out of there without killing any of the Rat Hunters. Sure, I destroyed the home and all their belongings, but they don't need that anymore. Look on the bright side. You exceeded Charlie's expectations! When this is all over, I'm sure he'll be impressed.

Smirking, I get into the red dune buggy, start the battery, and take off, hoping the rest of this trip goes just as smoothly as this.

CHAPTER 5

NO STOPPING

ALI SCHOLTZ
DECEMBER 22, 2064

The ride to our entry point is only an hour, so I don't understand why Lady Black Hair is so fidgety.

"Are you sure this is safe?" she yells over the wind. "It looks like there's a lot of places people can jump out at us. And our car has no walls."

To be fair, she's right. We're easy pickings driving through the empty street. Most of the buildings are just skeletons made of metal, but there are some that have really good hiding spots.

There's really not much out here. Besides some random houses that still stand, the entire neighborhood is flat gray land. Literally, every building, standing or not, is gray. The road is gray, the ground is gray, and the sky is gray and super chilly and somehow dry at the same time. I don't know why, but the ground kinda sparkles as we drive over it.

"Hello?" Lady Black Hair yells at me again. Her voice is kinda deep and husky.

Is she sick?

As I speed through the abandoned town, I look into the small mirror above my head at her. "Hi!" I say enthusiastically. "Um, first we are in a dune buggy, and second we're basically here, so don't worry. The Wright Gang burnt down this place years ago after abandoning it." *Oh crap.* I sigh, realizing I shouldn't have said that.

"The Wright Gang?" yells Lady Black Hair. "Do you know what they do to people like us?"

"Well, uh, yeah. They're, um, bastards, but they haven't been here in years. Char ... ugh, my boss checked this place out yesterday, so we'll be okay."

Butterfly grabs Lady Black Hair's hand.

Way to go, Ali. Why not tell them this is your second run? And that the first group nearly died? Why not say most people die in the Labyrinth? I'm sure they'll enjoy another one of your fantastic scares. I need to say something to lighten their mood.

"Hey, have you ever heard of this thing called a knock-knock joke?"

The family shake their heads, confused where I'm going with this.

"Well," I say smiling, "when I say, 'knock-knock,' you say, 'who's there?' Then I say something, and you say it again, then say 'who,' and then I say the punchline. You get it?" I look in the mirror. The family is still very confused. "Okay," I say, ignoring their confused faces. "Let's just do it. Ready?"

"Ready!" says the young girl. *Thank you!* "That's the spirit! Knock, knock."

"Who's there?" she responds, now smiling.

"Adore."

"Adore who?"

Hey she got it! "Adore is between us! Open up!" I look behind me, smiling, expecting other light grins. No one is laughing. *What? When I first heard a knock-knock joke, I thought it was the funniest thing ever. Now, they're pretty meh, but still! Just gotta brush it off and try again.*

"Oh, you didn't like that one. Oh, okay. I see. Guess I gotta step up my game then. Knock, knock."

"Who's there?" says Butterfly. *Maybe she's enjoying it.*

"A leaf."

"A leaf who?" yells back the little boy. He's now sitting up in his seat. His eyes sparkling with excitement.

Hell yeah! "A leaf you alone, if you leaf me alone!"

The little boy starts laughing. So, does the little girl. Lady Black Hair tries to hide her smile. *Yay, it's working!*

"Oh, can I try one?" yells back the son.

"Of course, anyone can try one. But the real question is, are you any good?"

"I'm better than you!" he yells back.

Wow, cocky much? "Well, bring it on, big man, let me see what you got."

He stops for a moment and starts thinking.

We arrive at the signal for the entry point. There's the rusty car in front of the house. Unlike the rest, this one is neatly parked on the side of the road and has a pink *X* painted on it. The others are either flipped over or have green or white markings on them. The clock reads. 11:36. *We've got time.* I take my foot off the pedal and cruise so that the kid can tell his joke. The dune buggy slows down.

"Knock, knock," he says, squeaking.

"Who's there?"

"Candice."

Butterfly shoots the boy a look. *Her name must be Candice. Oh crap.* I step back on the pedal.

"Candice, who?"

"Candice thing go any faster?"

Wow, what an amateur. Time to force a laugh. I start laughing loudly. His sister rolls her eyes, obviously not impressed. Candice, no, Butterfly laughs as well. So does Lady Black Hair.

"Wow, you are a natural," I say through my forced laugh.

"Yeah, Jake," says Lady Black Hair, "maybe you can be one of those funny actors we hear about."

Jake? Are they trying to break my rules?

"Really? You think so," he says, satisfied.

"Of course, sweetie," Lady Black Hair says and ruffles up his dirty blond hair.

"We're here," I say, interrupting the love fest. *I can't be so nice to them anymore. Soon, I'll learn all their names, and Charlie's gonna be pissed cuz imma do something stupid.*

Much like the surrounding homes, the entry point's house is not in great shape. The roof is partially collapsed, crushing what would've been a fence. The walls are faded, but they look like they were blue? Maybe. I can't really tell.

Slowing down, so I don't blow a tire, I drive over the collapsed roof into the backyard. It is pretty small. There's a pool in the corner filled with black water. Behind it is our entry point. An old fallout shelter with its massive metal door and concrete frame. A big yellow nine is painted on the cover, and next to that, the Wright Gang's red falcon.

Is Barry still down here? I haven't seen him in years! Ugh, I can't wait to show him all the new moves I learned in training.

Standing next to the shelter is the Charon. He wears all black clothing and a black face covering. I pull down my arm and show him my tattoo. He does the same.

"Okay, up up," I say as I hop out of the buggy. When I land, the dust puffs around my feet. I grab my backpack and sling it over my body. I start walking to the entry point when the Charon stops me and points. I turn around. The family is still in the buggy.

Lady Black Hair looks at me and scoffs, "What do you mean, 'up up'? You mean we're not taking the car?"

Really, how many times do I have to say it? "Dune buggy," I say agitatedly, "And no, we go underground to get into the city. Otherwise, we get … yeah." *Good job. Way to avoid the killed word.*

The family slowly gets out of the buggy. As they do, the Charon jumps in and drives off.

Now it's just them and me. Don't mess this up. No need to repeat last time's errors. Turn one leads to a gun, turn right, and you'll be all right. Go straight to the count of thirty-two, or else get skewered by three dudes. Pause and wait to the count of eight, or else turn to a slab of bait. Dodge the …

"So, what now?" asks Lady Black Hair. "Now, you stay close to me and follow everything I do. That's basically the only rule to this. Oh, and no screaming. It's just a pet peeve."

"Easy enough," says Lady Black Hair. She turns back to the kids and talks to them. I can't hear what she's saying, but it doesn't matter.

The small keypad next to the door by the fallout shelter is dirty and really retro. *Who uses keypads anymore?* I type in the code, and the door screeches open loudly. After ten seconds of loud, sharp noises, the door stops. I turn back to the family, who stare at me in disbelief.

"Okay, I can see why you're worried," I say to them calmly, "but there's no reason to be. The rest of the trip will be a lot quieter than this."

Jake has a tiny granola bar. Delicious, but he's definitely gonna get us killed down there. "Hey, so uh, Jake," I say and walk up to him with a smile, "you can't bring any food with you in there. Definitely get rid of that." Jake looks at me so sad. *No, stay strong.* "Sorry, buddy, but we don't want to leave any trace we were here unless we have to and ..." Jake's eyes seem to grow bigger than his head. *I really gotta learn to talk less. Note to self: Think before saying anything ever again.* "Just leave it behind, okay?" I say calmly and as nicely as I possibly can. Jake stares at his mom for support, but she got my message pretty clearly.

"Will you be okay without any food for a while?" Candice asks the kids.

"Yes, mom," says the little girl. "We'll be fine."

"I'm actually kind of hungry still," Jake whimpers. His sister punches him in the arm. "Ow!" Jake screams. "What the heck!"

Lady Black Hair tells off her daughter, "Now Nancy, if your brother wants to eat, we let him eat. We have time to rest, don't we uh ..." Lady Black Hair stares at me.

What does she want? Why is she staring at me? Oh yeah.

"Sorry, I can't tell you my name. You know, safety concerns. And about the breaks," I say and look at my watch: 11:47, "we can't have that either. We have a very small window to make it through all the security, so a break now will definitely lessen our chances to, um, none. And leave the food behind. Bury it, actually. Don't want anyone tracking us."

The family just looks so sad. Little Jake is slumped over. Nancy leans against Lady Black Hair. Candice looks at the ground.

Why do they look so sad? They're like ten minutes away from paradise. The last group I led, maybe if they had any sort of inspiration, they could've made it through easier. Ah, to hell with what Charlie said, we're not making it through this if I'm just a nameless guide. They need some motivation now, so I'll give it to them.

"All right, my name is Ali Scholtz. I am nineteen years young, and I'm gonna lead you to paradise safely. Jake, Nancy, Candice, and Lady Black Hair—"

"Heather," Lady Black Hair interrupts.

"Right, and Heather. I am taking you to start a new life in a place taken away from you. Now, you've earned your spot there just by surviving out here for this damn long." I look at the kids, "Pardon the language. Better get used to it. And now, you have one last challenge, a pretty easy one, actually, before you can get to paradise. You ready to kick its ass?"

Heather smiles and hugs her wife. "Let's do it," she says happily.

Man, I should be a speechwriter. Gotta talk to Charlie about that when I get back. "All right then. Do what I say, and we'll be so fine. Paradise awaits!"

With that absolutely bonkers speech, together as a new temporary, everlasting family, we enter Barry's fallout shelter. It's really dark since the only light is coming from outside. The inside of the shelter is all metal and is like an icebox because it's so cold outside. It's also really small, so only Nancy and Jake can stand up straight. There are a couple of empty water jugs sitting next to—

"Barry!" I scream. I grab the skeleton from the mattress he lies on. He still has all his limbs intact and no damages to his bones. "Okay, before we leave," I say enthusiastically, "this is Barry. I found him in a school a couple of years ago before my first run. Ah, I don't know why, but he's so cool. He's just someone you can really connect with, you know?" The family stares at me, concerned like I'm crazy. *They probably think he's actually a real skeleton. Like from a human.* "Oh, ha ha, you think he's real," I say through a half-laugh. "He's not actually real, like he's not from a human. He's made of eco-decomposable material."

"You mean biodegradable?" asks Heather, still confused.

Great job, Ali. Charlie told you to stop using big words that I can't possibly understand. Now I look like an idiot. "Oh yeah, obviously," I respond, brushing off her challenge, "I have a stutter, you know, so …" *Really, lying? New low.* I drop Barry disappointed. *Sorry, buddy. Looks like I really haven't changed that much.*

The stopwatch in my pocket goes off, saving me from more embarrassment. I turn off the orange stopwatch and pocket it, then say, "Okay, you guys ready?" The family nods. "Cool, from now on, not a single word. Okay?" They nod. *It's now my job to get them through here alive. Don't psych yourself out. Stay calm. Everything will come naturally.*

I push away the mattress and show the tunnel. A cool breeze flows out and hits my face. Looking down into the darkness, I set my timer for thirty-two seconds. *It's now my job to get them through here alive. Just do what you do best: run.* Taking a deep breath, I take my first step down.

"Wait," Heather calls back from behind me, "you're armed, right? In case we have to… you know …" Her voice trails off, and she glances at the kids.

Deep breath. You've prepared for this sorta thing.

"You see this timer right here?" I say calmly, trying to change my voice to Charlie's more serious one. I pull out the timer from my pocket and show Heather. "If I don't get you to a certain spot before this timer runs out, we are not going to make it. If you don't want to continue with me, that fine. The closest populated place is about a ten-mile walk northeast of here. I can escort you there, but our odds of surviving those ten miles are very small cuz of the Wright Gang. So, leave now or come with me and escape Nowhere. Your choice."

I wait for a response.

Heather looks at Candice. They have one of those silent conversations I never could get the hang of, then look at me and nod. *Wow. Note to self: changing tone really helps.* "Now seriously," I say, using the same tone, "no talking." The family nods again. Nancy drags her fingers across her lips and then twists her fingers at the end of her mouth. *What does that mean? I'll ask her when we get inside.* Together, we walk down the tunnel into the darkness.

CHAPTER 6

THE PYRAMID

JIMMY MARSHALL
DECEMBER 22, 2064

On the screen implanted into the conference room wall of Good Life Enterprises' office, I rotate through G.L.E. Square's security footage.

He can't be a no-show today.

On the screen lies the moving image of the Square. Hundreds of people swarm the gray watered lawns dressed in their colorful clothing. Some play basketball on the outdoor courts.

"Circe," I ask aloud.

"Yes, sir?" the AI's voice responds through the walls of the conference room. Her two chimes remind me of sleigh bells on Christmas Eve.

"Search G.L.E. Square for Usof Mendoza," I command.

Circe's two chimes commence, and the screen rapidly scans the location. The image flips to another camera, then another, and third.

How can he not be here today?

Finally, the screen stills. The image scans a lone man on a bench. He sits with synthetic flowers. His long, curly brown hair at his shoulders. He wears a $300 Fasano polo, $220 Day dress jeans, and his $510 Splotassi dress shoes. A $7,000 ring sits heavy in his pocket. His heart beats at 110 beats per minute.

A woman approaches wearing a $170 sundress. "Circe, remove the statistics and find a more cinematic angle. I want to enjoy this moment." Her two chimes echo in the conference room.

The image shifts to a near silhouette of Usof and Julie sitting on the bench. The sunset reflects on a nearby pond. The city's skyscraper's lining up like the beautiful concrete jungle I imagined they would be.

"Do you have any self-awareness?" the screeching voice of Elani shakes me to the core. My neck tightens as I turn to face the CEO of Goof Life Enterprises. Her dark skin and maple eyes clash with her tacky blond hair. Her low-cut suit top and tight skirt are highly inappropriate for a meeting of this urgency.

Bite your tongue.

"It's not like you have never watched the citizens interact, Elani. I'm actually invested in their well-being."

"Ha! Of course, Jimmy," her squeaking voice quips, "Whatever you say. You don't have to lie, you know. This isn't one of your rallies."

If she calls me Jimmy one more time …

"Let's get to it, Elani," I spit before I slip an insult I cannot recover from, "What's this grand emergency you wanted to discuss?" Elani walks across the conference room and sits at the table only a foot away. She grabs two playing cards from her coat pocket and places them in front of me. One is the Queen of Hearts. The other is the Queen of Diamonds. The image on the screen changes to thin blue lines of a pyramid.

"Another crisis?" I ask.

"Beyond," her wavering voice stammers, "This has the ability to completely destroy our hold over the Paradise Cities."

She's so dramatic.

"What?" I ask sarcastically, "Is it the end of the world?"

"For us," her voice is different. She's typically exaggerative, but this is unusually desperate.

At the top floor of G.L.E.'s fishhook-shaped building, I can see beyond the wall into Nowhere. The quiet desert even shines with the sunset, turning its gray and ashy terrain a hint of orange. The window tints and the conference room darkens. On the far side, the haunting image of my skinny, paranoid former engineer lights the room.

"Levi O'Scandrick has finally decided to bring an end to the peace in the Paradise Cities. He's planning on telling—"

I choke on air.

"Don't you finish that sentence! You know better than to speak of that in a place so open!"

Elani migrates to the screen. She waves her hand in front of it, revealing the Pyramid made in case such an instance occurred.

"It's time, Jimmy," she continues, her voice shaken, "we have to implement Levi's Pyramid."

This doesn't make sense. He knows our deal. He knows what'll happen to …

"How did you find out about this?"

"His wife, Kaiya, as well as their friends Javier and Aisling Jones have decided to release the information on Joe's live *Late Show* tonight. An informant says that Aisling is planning to show a clip. We did some digging, along with those at Tigress, and saw Aisling and Kaiya have somehow severed their connection to G.L.E. servers and have not used any Tigress tech for the past six months."

"You're basing this accusation—this death sentence on that? Are you serious, Elani?"

"There's one more thing. Your Leo said Joe's planning to bring Levi on as a surprise guest. Apparently, he's planning 'something big' for Levi. If they successfully expose us—"

"Just cancel the show today then!" I interrupt, "Figure out a way to pin it on Levi. That's enough of a warning to keep him bedridden for weeks."

"We've already canceled the show. But they'll just go and find another way to distribute the information, especially with Levi on their side. They're too dangerous. *He's* too dangerous for us. If this gets out there, we'll lose control of the masses. They'll see us as traitors instead of saviors."

Her cold, near emotionless delivery sends a shiver down my spine. This fool, does he really think he can do this? And getting his wife involved? That doesn't sound like him at all.

I stare at the cards on my desk. Both Queens mock me. The wrinkled face of the Queen of Diamonds catches my eye. The clean look of the Queen of Hearts …

"Circe!" I yell at the AI, "Send in Leo 8, please. Fill him in. I want his opinion on the matter immediately."

"Of course, sir," Circe responds.

Elani's dark face is stoic. Her eyes show no worry. Her face shows no stress.

She's a showman. Panicking to get a rise out of me. She already made up her mind. She just needs my approval.

"And you are sure he is going to break his deal?" I ask, a lump forming in my throat, "That he's going to lose everything?"

Elani focuses on the Pyramid. On the conservative face, she adjusts the AI reporter, already writing the animated anchorman his script for the fallout.

"Let me put it this way for you, Jimmy," her voice says. "Do you really want to take that risk? Do you really want to lose this city?"

Leo enters the conference room. His fiery red hair doesn't match his emotionless gray eyes. He scans the room, locking onto the Pyramid. "Good," he says in his monotone voice, "I'll start today." He approaches the pyramid, his hands behind his back as he walks.

Levi's and my rules of the Pyramid appear on screen, along with scribbles of its first usage from six years ago:

STEP 1: FIND DESPERATE PEOPLE OR PEOPLE WITH NO HOPE. THOSE WHO FEEL THEY HAVE BEEN WRONGED BY SOCIETY (TRULY OR FALSE).

STEP 2: RECOGNIZE THEIR PAIN AND GIVE THEM SOME TRUTH ABOUT THEMSELVES NO ONE HAS RECOGNIZED (UNSPOKEN TRUTH—IT'S REAL, BUT ONLY PART OF THE STORY). "I RECOGNIZE YOUR PAIN AND WILL GIVE YOU A VOICE."

STEP 3: CREATE AN ENEMY (LEVI). MANUFACTURE LIES ABOUT THE ENEMY TO GIVE YOU POWER. MORE FEAR EQUALS MORE POWER.

STEP 4: DON'T LET THEM SEE ANYTHING YOU DON'T KNOW ABOUT. CONTROL THE INFO, CONTROL THEIR MINDS, CONTROL THEIR LOYALTY. CREATE A STATE OF RELIANCE AND REJECTION OF OPPOSITION (STRIKE A DEAL WITH G.L.E.)

STEP 5: REPEAT UNTIL FACT IS FICTION, AND YOUR WORD IS THE ONLY TRUTH. DO SO FOR THE FOUR SIDES OF SOCIETY, EACH A SIDE OF THE PYRAMID: LIBERAL, CONSERVATIVE, AMDIVALENT, AND HELPLESS.

On the top of the outline reads, "When the system fails the people, we, the desperate, turn to the best, the fastest, the loudest measures to win what we require to live," Levi O'Scandrick.

My mind takes me back to that day. We are in the nearly complete Paradise City: Denver standing inside G.L.E.'s headquarters. My suit was still covered in mud. The original Leo still standing by my side. And Levi in his oversized jeans and shaved head.

"You realize if he quits, we're screwed," Leo's panicky voice squeaks.

I hold up my hand and silence him.

The People's Republic of Russia and China's dual presidents watch over us from their home countries. Their faces cover the massive floor-to-ceiling screens.

"And you're sure your plan will ensure no one will know what's happened here ever transpired?" I ask Levi.

"Of course. Building the Paradigm Pyramid with strong stones like this will allow for the greatest of lies to last for generations. Once set, it's hard to get rid of. People won't change their minds."

"You sound very confident for a man on the verge of death," the Russian president taunts Levi.

"I'm not nearly close to death," Levi answers, his voice confident despite his shaking body, "And I won't ever be close because I will never say a word. Even if I did, nothing I know can combat this system. Whatever I do will be lost in the Pyramid." He turns to me, smirking as if he's won, "When the system fails the people, we, the desperate, turn to the best, the fastest, the loudest measures to win what we require to live. Whatever it takes."

The Chinese President waves his hand. A robotic officer, a mere prototype back then, drugs Levi. He collapses into its arms.

"We have made our deal," I quickly say before the heads of the P.R.R.C. can give the kill order, "He has given us what we needed. From now on, we are in control."

Returning from my memory. My body stings. The shame, nearly unbearable.

The windows in the conference room lose their tint. Outside, the sunset over the city paints the sky with streaks of orange, purple, and blue. It reflects off the top of The Dome, giving the tinted glass monstrosity some much needed color. The wall sparkles from the rush of nature's most outstanding colors, crowning it with a halo. Below me, thousands of people continue to move through the city. Murals on the street celebrating all the mixed cultures that created this perfect home. All these people, given everything they need not to just live, but thrive.

I bring my scene from earlier into view on the table. In the apartments above the Hispanic Youth Center, Circe finds Usof and Julie looking out of their eleventh-floor apartment window at the setting sun. A new diamond ring on her finger.

Elani catches me staring at my screen. "That's quite a view," she says, a smug grin streaking across her smooth face.

I grab the Queen of Diamonds and hold it in my shaking hand.

Taking a deep breath, I sigh. My heartbeat slows as the air leaves my lungs.

Whatever it takes.

"It sure is."

CHAPTER 7

INTO THE LABYRINTH

ALI SCHOLTZ
DECEMBER 22, 2064

The Labyrinth is a lot different than I remember. Two years ago, it was all white, and there were lights and cameras everywhere. I had to wear special camouflage that made us invisible to the security cams. Now, it's sorta a dump.

The farther we get from Barry's shelter, the darker the tunnels get. I can barely see a thing, and I can't whip out my flashlight without getting spotted. There are only a few flickering bulbs that line the left brick wall, and they're not even LED. The floor is dirt instead of marble, but it's rock hard like they pressed it together too tightly. My breath breaks through the dark light. About fifteen seconds in, we approach the first intersection. It's straight ahead, about fifty meters.

Turn one leads to a gun, turn right, and you'll be all right.

As we get closer, there's the all-too-familiar hum of fusion batteries approaching to my right. There's no way they're down here. Just to be safe, I gesture for the family to stop and lie down. I do the same on my stomach. I look up and see lights coming right at us. Less than a second later, three motorbikes fly past. On them, three soldiers wearing a white uniform with a red falcon etched into the shoulder.

How the hell did the Wright Gang get down here? Charlie didn't tell me about this.

This messes up my every move. They came from the right, and I'm supposed to go right after the first intersection. Well, since they went left, that means that's their headquarters or something, right? *Exactly, see, Charlie knew what he was doing.* I get up, and the family follows. *Go straight to the count of thirty-two, or else get skewered by three dudes.*

Turning right, I start my timer to the count of thirty-two. I begin my slow jog to make up for the time lost thinking. This tunnel is a lot different than the other. On the ceiling are the remains of the old tunnel mixed in with the ugliness of the new one. The silver ceiling reflects the little bit of light left.

The family seems so calm. Jake is holding Candice's hand. Heather is behind them, and Nancy is on my heels, leading the way for the group. I smile.

There are eight seconds left on the timer. *I guess we have to stop before this next intersection.* I gesture for the family to stop. They do and lie down even before I do. The timer ends, and I reset it.

Pause and wait to the count of eight, or else turn to a slab of bait. As we lie on the dirt floor, I mouth to myself the eight count. *One, two, three. Nothing's there. Four, five. C'mon, where's this thing. Six, seven.* Out of nowhere, a massive six-wheeled pickup truck drives past us, barely even making a sound. *Eight. Holy crap, that thing's ridiculously quiet. Dodge the space, or else a ball will drop posthaste.*

I stand up and look for any particular cracks or crevices. Although it's dark, a section of the ground is lifted higher than the rest. *Thank you eyes.* I gesture for the family to follow right behind me. They nod. I line up on the right side of the wall, opposite the slightly raised space. They follow.

Slowly inching forward, we cross the intersection. The floor on the other side is marble. Beautiful and white like it used to be. The bad news is our steps echo down the halls. We're not wearing the cushioned shoes like I had last time.

Okay, plus minus. Plus, I can hear people coming. Minus, they hear me coming. At least it'll be fair enough for them. I snicker a little at my cockiness. *What's the next section? Oh, the next road has the key. Just get it on fourteen and person three.*

I set the timer for fourteen seconds. Quietly we continue forward. Our footsteps create a soft echo in the tunnel. This part of the tunnel is much more lit than the rest. The wall on the right has a mirror on it. The family walks slowly behind me, with Nancy leading the way.

Why would they put a mirror in a tunnel? Then a light turns on behind it. *Nope! It's a window!* I dive to the ground as the lights in the neighboring room turn on. The family does the same. *Note to self: if one side of a window is dark and the other side is light, a window can be a mirror too.*

There are only ten seconds left on the timer. Quickly, I take a peek through the window to see if anyone noticed us. Nope, but inside is a woman in a lab coat. She has a baby in her arms. Placing the baby on a metal table, the woman gives the baby a toy.

Ah, cute.

As the baby plays with the toy, the woman presses a tiny red button next to the metal table. As she does so, the baby starts screaming. Then, almost as fast as she put the baby down, she lifts it up.

Ah! Not cute!

On the back of the baby, there's a large tattoo of a falcon. *Of course, it's the Wright Gang. Why are these guys everywhere? For once, why can't they just, I don't know, not be the worst?* In front of me, headlights approach. My timer ended. *This is exactly what Charlie warns me about. Don't get distracted. Stay focused. Three means there are three soldiers in this car. Smoke to not draw attention, then trank them.*

As the headlights get closer, I guess it's a military truck. The three soldiers I'm supposed to eliminate stare directly at me. I wave at them just cuz. They continue to stare, confused. Wearing their green camouflage (which really doesn't make sense since we're, you know, underground), they approach slowly.

I tap the right tube on my backpack. Pin out, a smoke grenade drops smoothly into my hand. I throw it at the truck, and smoke fills the air. The squeak of the truck's brakes echoes down the tunnel. As the smoke thickens, I open my backpack and grab the tranquilizer darts.

Somewhere in the smoke, a light voice says, "They're here. Find them." *Wait, how'd they know we're coming? No, stop thinking. Get the thumb.* The doors open, and the sound of the two separate pairs of combat boots hits the marble floor. *Two? Where's the third?*

A small part of the smoke in front of me moves. Grabbing one of the tranquilizer darts from my pocket, I approach the first soldier. As I get closer, the smoke around him spins faster, allowing me to see him clearly. Quietly, I sneak up from behind and stab him in the neck with the dart. The man doesn't make a sound as the tranquilizer's effect hits him immediately. I place him down without a sound.

The other soldier approaches from behind. His eyes get huge as I grab him. For less than a second, we make eye contact. I grin so he can sleep to a smiling face. *Or is that creepy?* Before he can react, I stick my second dart into his neck. I lay him down gently. *But seriously, where's the third?*

The family is now standing behind me. Their hands are over their mouths. I gesture for them that the smoke is okay to breathe. Slowly, they remove their hands.

"Wow, that was close," whispers Jake. Nancy shushes him loudly. Candice kneels and whispers something into her kids' ears. Jake looks sad as his mom stands back up. Nancy's smug. As I adore the two kids for being too adorable, Heather waves frantically at me. She points to the truck.

Mumbled, as if speaking through a wall, is the third guard. He's inside the truck, trying to radio in the attack. *Wow, maybe Heather should be a coyote.* Approaching the car, I hear the soldier repeatedly saying, "Hello? Does anyone copy?" The hot metal of the car burns my hand as I grab the handle. When I open the door, the baby-faced guard looks at me with bug eyes. Before he can reach for his gun, I stab him in the neck with my third dart. He passes out instantly.

That was easy enough. Now the keys.

I rip the badge off the soldier's uniform. Then, sticking my hand into his pocket, I find his tiny plastic ID card. I slide it into my pocket.

Now, for the fun part. Pulling out my knife, I grab the soldier's hand to separate the thumb from the rest.

"Ali," Nancy says from behind. Her eyes are big and stuck.

Oh, I probably should've told her not to look. "Hey, um, you might want to, you know, turn around for this one. Sorry," I say, trying to stay lighthearted. Nancy continues to stare for a second, then looks up at me. The hurt in her eyes is too much. She turns around and disappears into the smoke. *I'm sorry, Nancy, but this is the only way through. Why does everything have to be so violent? Why can't he just have a secret password instead of a thumbprint?* I cut off the soldier's thumb. Taking off his camo arm bandanna, I stuff the thumb into it.

I whisper-yell out to the family, "All right, sorry you had to see that. It's horrible this is what is required to get you guys a better life. But we need to jog to the next place if we actually want to make it out. So just stay close together, and we'll be fine, cool?" The family follows my voice and appears in the smoke. Heather nods as she hugs Nancy.

Shit. Why'd she have to see that?

I can't comfort her. We don't have the time. Instead, I take off to our next destination. This whole fight could've been avoided probably took away a couple of seconds, meaning we can expect company when we get to the door.

What's the next line? Ignore the turns to avoid the burns. Instead, head straight to the comfy B.E.D. by the count of twenty-eight.

With the timer set for twenty-eight seconds, I speed up to reach our destination on time. The tunnel ahead of us is much narrower than the rest. I don't think a normal-sized car could get in here, let alone those massive military trucks. The marble floor has changed into concrete, making the echo from before disappear. As we continue, the tunnel shrinks. The ceiling keeps getting smaller, and the floor and walls look like they've collapsed. There are multiple turns along the way to bigger areas, but like the rhyme said, *head straight*.

Then, of course, we reach a split in the road, where both areas are technically going straight. The right one curves a little to the right, but the one on the left side curves slightly left but is straighter. But the right one is more in line with me, so I don't have to technically turn.

I can't slow down, or else we'll definitely miss entry, so Imma say right. Please be right. As I continue to run, I notice the left floor flicker. A little blue wave moves across the floor with lightning speed. *It's a false floor. Great instincts, Ali. Great instincts.* I'm barely able to stand as we reach the B.E.D.

CHAPTER 8

THE LABYRINTH

ALI SCHOLTZ
DECEMBER 22, 2064

The Blocked Entry Door is a large stone engraved with a big bald eagle. There are two scanners. One for the finger and one for the badge, plus a code. Taking out the badge and the severed thumb, I scan them both at once. The scanners light up green. The ground shakes as the stone eagle splits in half, revealing the keypad. I type in the ridiculously long code. When I finish, the rest of the B.E.D. opens with the same loud rumble.

As the door opens slowly, dust falls from the ceiling. Then pebbles. Then rocks.

Walls are collapsing. No wonder this tunnel is so small. It can barely hold itself up.

Grabbing Jake, who was conveniently right next to me, I dive through the barely opened door. Heather, Nancy, and Candice follow just in the nick of time. The tunnel collapses. The door is now half-opened with a large boulder holding it in place.

I stand up to take inventory. We're in the middle of really old subway tracks. We have all the members of the family.

Nancy has a cut on her elbow. Candice looks fine, just dirty. Heather has a bunch of dirt in her thick, curly hair. Jake sniffles up tears. His whimpers echo down the subway tunnel.

"Hey, Jake," I say and kneel next to him, "you okay?"

"I'm scared," Jake shouts, "I want to go home!" Crying loudly.

Crap. C'mon Jake. Pull it together. We're so close.

"Jake, we can't do that, buddy," I say quietly. "We're so close to your new home. It's just, 'down the final tunnel you'll turn, to the paradise you've earned.'" The family stares at me, confused. "What? Rhyming helps," I respond, embarrassed. Heather hugs Jake, who jumps into his mom's arms and hides his face in her shoulder. She looks at me, concerned. Then in a calm voice asks, "Where to next?"

How come they're so sad? Yeah, it's a scary tunnel, but they're so close to getting in. Shouldn't they be happy?

"This way," I say, now feeling down. Heather looks at me, shaken, then follows. Same with the rest of the family.

The gigantic tunnel is empty and must reach about fifteen meters high and probably ten meters wide. The tracks are covered with gravel and other random objects. Despite the subway having no lights, at the end, there's a lot of light. Super bright.

We're no more than twenty meters away from the station when the scenery changes. The right wall is a mountain of rubble. Beneath that pile is an old subway car. Its windows have been shattered, and its white and blue paint chips and falls off its body.

As we get closer to the actual platform, there are quiet, mumbling voices echoing down the tunnel. A woman and a man yell about something. I can't quite make it out.

Still standing on the tracks, I pop my head above the platform. Another soldier. His all-black uniform blends into the shadow of the pillar he's standing under. On the left side, stairs lead up to Little Village seventeen. I duck back down to avoid getting spotted.

We're so close! Why can't these things just be easy? Okay, so what's next. Ignore the turns to avoid the burns. Instead, head straight to the comfy B.E.D. by the count of twenty-eight. Down the final tunnel, you'll turn to the paradise you've earned. Then ... wait, that's it? There's no more? Dammit!

I look back up over the ledge. There's the guard hiding in the shadows of the nearest pillar. *Okay, so that's one.* Another sits on the staircase. *That's two.* Moving right, there's blood on the concrete. *Ignore that. Actually, don't ignore that. White tile floor plus liquid equals slippery. Avoid or lead soldiers into them.* One of the four pillars in the station has collapsed. The one farthest from me holds up the incomplete second story, and it looks weak. There are cracks in it, and the top of the pillar is missing a good chunk.

"What? You seriously think I can't shoot the light off that train?" A woman's voice yells, making a loud echo throughout the station. She sits on the weak second-story structure with a sniper rifle. Her golden hair is tied back into a ponytail.

"Hell no," says a man in a deep voice. He is a big, big guy. His M16 rifle looks tiny in his dark hands.

"Fine," the woman responds, "put twenty bucks on it." The giant grunts and doesn't respond.

The sniper scoffs, "Wow, okay. What's gotten into you?"

"Nothing. I don't like betting with you. Every time we put money on something, you don't miss."

"Oh please, stop being such a wimp! It's a good football field away. Plus, I would have to make it through the little gaps in the rocks on top."

I continue to scan the station. Three spotlights line the second story. As they flash around, they create temporary shadows in the corners of the station. They even darken the shadow the first soldier stands in.

If only I can get him to move away. Five other soldiers stand on the platform, including two police bots. *Crap, not these things again.*

"Fine," the giant finally responds, "fifty bucks. No higher than that."

The sniper scoffs, "Cheap." Taking aim, she shoots. The loud bang of the rifle hurts my ears. The light in the subway car, well … it's gone. The sniper looks up from her scope then smiles at the big man.

"I'll give it to you when we're done with shift," he says.

"Dumbass," she mumbles to herself.

Well damn. So don't even risk getting spotted. Got it. Behind the subway car is a crack, revealing the gray dirt of Nowhere. *Bleh, I gotta find a better name for our home. What's wrong with New, New, New York? It's catchy. But more importantly, I can use that as our diversion. A place as well guarded as this definitely knows about that little hole.*

I turn back to the family. So sad. I mean, even Nancy's head is hung. I gesture for them to move backward, so our whisper chat doesn't echo. Jake is whimpering again. His cries are not going to help us right now. Those police will not hesitate to kill him.

"Okay, little guy, I mean man. Big, big man," I whisper. "I need you to take charge for me, okay? So, can you do that? Can you get your sister and mamma safe?"

Jake shakes his head.

Really? "Okay, uh, Nancy can—" I can't even finish my question before she grabs her brother's hand and puffs out her chest. *Hell yeah!* "Okay now, Candice, I know you still have that hammer. Take it out now, and don't be afraid to use it."

Wait, what if she gets too aggressive and attacks when she shouldn't?

"Scratch that. Be afraid to use it. Well, not afraid, just don't unless you need to. Nancy, take this timer. When you reach the shadow under the pillar directly in front of us, press start." I point to the top left button. Nancy hugs the timer to her chest, obviously happy with the responsibility.

"Heather, just make sure Jake is okay. When I do my thing, make a run for the staircase. Your new clothes are in the women's bathroom in the monorail station. I'll meet you outside in one minute. If I don't, uh, well, I hope you enjoyed my service and live your best lives. Oh, and wash up in the bathroom really quick, so you can get your smell off you."

Heather looks at me, offended. "What, apparently, we have a smell." Heather's eyes widen as footprints thud behind us.

I turn around only to find the soldier from the pillar now on our level. Pushing the family, we lie down behind the platform. "Hey, Brady. What you doing?" the giant man asks.

"I thought I heard something," Brady responds in a Boston accent.

"You didn't hear jack shit, man. It's the boredom playing tricks on you, man." Brady's footsteps get louder as he approaches our hiding spot.

I pull out a tranquilizer dart from my pocket. I grip it repeatedly.

"Brady, get your ass back up here," the giant man yells. Brady's footsteps stop, about a meter away from us. After a moment, he turns around and yells, "Fine. But if I get chewed out for missing something, I'm blaming yo' ass."

"Ha," the big man laughs, "we'll see about that."

"Wanna bet?" asks the sniper. Before Brady can even react, I sneak up behind him and stab him in the neck with a dart. Covering his mouth with my hand, I muffle his scream. For a moment, he tries to fight, but the drug takes over, and his body completely relaxes. I lay him down gently on the ground.

No reaction from the other guards. Not even the bots are on us yet.

How am I gonna get a distraction good enough to be worthwhile but not get the family killed?

I take another peek at the structure on the second story. The giant man paces over to the other side, and the small metal bars holding up the second story sway. If I take down the second story, that will cause the humans to freak out. The robots will come right at me, but at least the humans will be distracted. But I need explosives.

The now unconscious one named Brady is a standard soldier, and given the fact that these soldiers never see any action, I bet he still has two hurt grenades on his belt. Taking his thumb, I place it on the black box where the grenades are kept, unlocking it. *Three* grenades fall out into my hand.

Okay, so I can use the first for the second story. The second can go onto the first police robot that comes at me. The third to seal the door behind me. Sounds good.

I look back at the family and, waiting for the spotlight to swing away, gesture for them to get into position. Nancy presses start on the timer, then leads her family to the shadows. I set the first hurt grenade for fifteen and press Start. I then set the other two for contact impact. The first grenade displays seven, six, five, four. I throw it at the pillar, then the second at the nearest police robot. It latches on, and before the sniper can scream, the grenades explode, taking down the pillar and blowing up the robot officer.

The entire second story slowly collapses, taking down the surprised sniper and the giant man. As the explosion finishes off the second level, Nancy leads the family to the door. The soldier on the stairs doesn't even have time to recover before Candice swings her hammer and hits him in the chest. He collapses on the floor, gasping. The family runs up the stairs and disappears to the next level.

Mission complete.

As I run to the staircase, a bullet whizzes past my head. The sniper holds her pistol, her head bleeding into her golden hair. She can barely stand as her aim wobbles. Before I can react, she fires again, and a bullet cuts through my shoulder.

The pain is searing as if I'm getting burnt and stabbed all at once. My backpack strap snaps, and the pack falls to the ground. I fall with it. Before she can shoot again, I slide out of the pack and take out my knife, throw it, knocking the gun out of her hand. She yells a bloody roar and grabs her hand as my knife lands on the ground with a loud ping.

I take the last hurt grenade, and I throw it at the ceiling above the staircase. The soldier Candice took out rolls out of the way to avoid the explosion. I sprint toward the staircase. The loud echo of metal footsteps grows as the second robotic officer chases me down. Driving for the staircase, the hurt grenade explodes. The ceiling crumbles, taking the officer out with it.

I did it. I'm almost dead, but at least I did it. The family is safe. They are on the train heading into Paradise City: New York. Great job, me. Now I just have to get back out there without getting spotted. Easy.

I stand up from the staircase and examine my appearance. My shoulder hurts like all hell, and my chest does too. My white shirt is all torn up and soiled from dirt and blood.

So, so easy.

Climbing up the staircase, I enter the back of the ticket booth. The fake woman ticket robot lady thing is on the floor with her leg missing and her face smashed in. *Nice, Candice. No one's gonna notice that.* The red-tiled station is covered with people who, well, dress really nice. Everyone's clothes match perfectly. They're all so clean and ... all looking at me.

Oh yeah, the smell. And probably the blood.

On the monorail, the family stares at me from the front car. They're all cleaned up, new nonrainbow clothes and everything. Jake's still crying a bit, of course, but the rest of them look all right. I smile, then turn away. Don't want people seeing us together.

Over the speakers, a voice announces, "The doors are about to close." *Crap. I can't escape this place looking like this, and I got no time to change.* I run at a man on the phone, who isn't paying much attention, and grab the large gray coat dangling off his arm. I dive onto the monorail as the doors close.

Now that's an entrance!

I stand up from the ground and put the coat on, scanning the monorail for an empty seat. A strange looking, skinny white guy sits slumped over in a seat by himself. He has really sharp cheekbones and jaw. He looks like a skeleton. He's actively avoiding eye contact.

Is that Levi O'Scandrick? No, it's ... oh shit, it is! He's uglier in person than I thought. Is it worth making a scene to mock him? Yeah, it is. Just move cars at the next stop.

He squirms as I sit in the seat right next to him. *Oh, this is going to be fun. I should scare him!*

"Hey," he says in his squeaky voice. I don't respond. He stares at me, so scared it's hard to hold back a smile. However, before I brake, he turns his head away. I breathe a sigh of relief. Pulling out a piece of gum from my pocket, I unfold the wrapper. I then pull out the pen from my pocket.

What should I write to him? Hey, thanks for ruining our lives, you pig. Nah, too harsh. Rot in hell. Too bland. Maybe go to hell? Or is that too bland?

There's a fight outside of Modesto Park. It's just a minor fight, probably between the Wright Gang and Aiko's Freedom Gang. *I wonder if she's there.*

"Ugh," says a woman into her phone, "when are they going to put up that wall, so we don't have to see this crap." She stops complaining as a man yells something at her.

"Yeah, some bums just started shooting up the place! Yeah, Kyle. I'm fine."

What the hell? Does she not even care people are killing each other over scraps of food outside her wall. There's no way it's this bad. None of the other passengers are paying attention to the fight. *It's like we don't even matter. Charlie's right. These people deserve to be living out in Nowhere, not us.*

I write down on the wrapper, "Go to hell."

I turn to Levi, who is staring outside, actually kinda sad. His face frowns. His eyes hang down. *Don't tell me he's the only one who cares. Man, he's the bad guy. He did all this just so he could get rich. Yeah, there's no way he gives a damn.* But his face says otherwise. No … he's just like the rest. They don't even care if we die. Just don't die loudly, so we don't annoy their train time. Levi jumps back, startled that I was looking at him.

There's no way he cares.

"Sickening, isn't it?" I say calmly, trying to imitate Charlie's calm voice and words. "Another person blatantly avoiding the issue. It's like she doesn't care."

His face squishes together, confused, then he says, "Well, that's because she *doesn't* care."

Ha! He's just like the rest. "Yeah, well, she should, and so should you." Before he can react, I stuff my hand into his jacket pocket and place the wrapper in it. *He deserved worse. What was that thing Charlie said they call us? The Others? Please be right.*

"Remember the Others," I say.

Smirking, I head down to another car as the monorail stops. The doors open, and more people flood onto it, preventing me from seeing Levi's reaction.

I don't mind. I can't. Now I understand what Charlie really means. I can't mind his stupidity because we don't matter to him. We're not even people to them. No matter where we go, no matter what we do, we will be just another blip or loud noise in their lives. I just hope we can finally do right for the Other—no for the people around us. It's what we deserve.

CHAPTER 9

PARADISE CITY: NEW YORK

LEVI O'SCANDRICK
DECEMBER 22, 2064

Sitting on the monorail, I get to revisit the disgusting view of Nowhere. As my curiosity takes over, my fantasy starts to fade. Past the electrified fence that runs along the tracks like a cage in a zoo are the crumbled and ruined remains of prewar icons such as the Chrysler Building, whose pointed top juts out of the ground, no doubt providing shelter for the Others. Crumbling skyscrapers and other collapsed buildings appear in the distance through the fog.

What is the ecosystem of Nowhere? The Others get the full force of the sporadic weather, so how do they handle it? I would establish some sort of barrier between the people and me because we all know poverty leads to crime. So, create distance, find a building that isn't going to crumble on my head, and try to refurbish it. Maybe a factory. I would have power there if the backup generators are working. If not, I would have the tools to fix it.

Before long, we stop at the next station. As more citizens enter the monorail, so do the ads. They appear on the windows, blocking my view of Nowhere. One is a woman in a black jumpsuit with brown hair, olive skin, and brown eyes. Where she sits, an ad appears across from her for a discount at a gym. She must be Muslim because the model on the ad wears a hijab. There is a family with a teenage son with a fade haircut. Definitely an athlete. Their ad claims for the entire monorail to hear, "Look around you, life doesn't get any better than this, right? Sure it does! Here at G.L.E., we have one goal: give you The Good Life! So, before you get down in the dumps, remember to call G.L.E. We'll happily give you everything you need to be your best self. Here's to the Good Life!"

God, their ads suck.

As the doors close, a man jumps in the monorail, barely making it through. He is muscular, with a cut build. Blond, brown eyes, and dark skin. Around six feet tall. His sweat from running soaks through his white shirt and black suit jacket. His gray jeans are torn. He's out of breath, holding his hips as he walks toward me. Unlike the rest of the people on the monorail, he sits right next to me. He smells like rotting fish.

I focus on him, stunned but mostly just pissed off. His smug expression is directed forward, refusing to look me in the eye.

Were the rest of the seats on this monorail not good enough for you?

I don't want to make a scene, so I keep my thoughts to myself.

What is this guy's problem? Sure, he probably knows who I am and hates me, but really? Does he have to be so obvious about it? I stare daggers at the man, continuously hoping to engage in some sort of civil dialogue so I can get him to move. He just sits there like nothing's wrong. Why is he not even engaging with me? Something is wrong with this guy. Seriously wrong.

"Hey," I say to him, trying to restrain my anger. He doesn't engage. Looking forward. Not a word.

Why doesn't he answer me? Is he Marshall's spy? Maybe G.L.E.'s private police? No. Calm down. No more meltdowns. This day's the worst.

I look outside into Nowhere, hoping to get distracted. Further down the line, giant fields of solar panels line the fence, providing shade for those left on the outside of the wall. A complete waste of perfectly good technology. I could easily fix them and power an entire city with these, but no. Let the Others suffer. Crumbled houses and towns also line the tracks. As I ride past this set of homes, although I don't see it, there is a battle going on. Gunshots are fired.

"Ugh," says the woman in the black jumpsuit into her phone, "when are they going to put up that wall, so we don't have to see this crap?" She pauses as a muffled male voice comes out of her phone, then she answers, "Yeah, some bums just started shooting up the place! Yeah, Kyle. I'm fine."

I understand this is the world we live in. If only she knew what's really going on.

I turn toward the window only to find the blond man staring right at me. I jump back, startled.

"Sickening, isn't it?" he says in his smooth melancholy voice. "Another person blatantly avoiding the issue. It's like she doesn't care." He says that last sentence almost disappointed as if that weren't already obvious to him.

"Well, that's because she *doesn't* care," I respond matter-of-factly.

"Yeah, well, she should, and so should you." Before I realize it, his hand is in my jacket pocket.

"What the hell are you doing?" I screech and pull away, but it's too late. His grip is ironclad.

"Remember the Others," he says and heads to the doors. The monorail pulls into the second station. The blonde man walks off to another car and disappears into the crowd.

I pull the card out of my pocket and read it. Instead of some brochure, it's a crumbled piece of gum wrapper that says, "Go to hell," sloppily written on it. *Asshole.* I get up and throw the wrapper in the trash, only to turn around and find my seat taken. *Great. Absolutely fantastic.*

I sit next to the family. I mean, what was the point of that? Was he trying to send me a message? One of those "terrorists" I keep hearing about? I shiver thinking of that.

The monorail slowly pulls out of the station. It's already five o'clock. *Why are they moving so slow today? Are the batteries dying? Bet those solar panels would help.*

As we continue along the track, more familiar sites emerge behind the bright and colorful ads. SARR (Smog and Radiation Removal) machines line up along the border fence. Their massive tan brick bases, marked with the P.R.R.C.'s flag, match the color of the earth that surrounds them. Their three vents that line the top of the tan box base are covered in dust and filth. The SARR's are followed by more decaying towns and gray wasteland.

A few more people have joined me on the monorail. All of them have their noses inside their Tigress Glasses. All of them are so involved in their devices. Outside the window, a man is shot by a guard, and no one gives a damn. It's kind of funny to me. Usually, the government tries to hide their suspicious acts because of how aware people are of their surroundings, but now, it's almost like they can shoot a person in the street, and no one will bat an eye. People are so focused on removing themselves from reality that they just normalize certain events as if the headline said, "Humans have two eyes." Pathetic.

The majority of people are focused on their phones. A few have turned on the televisions in the windows of the monorail, blocking my view of the outside. There are around fifty people now in the car. About three-quarters are standing. If I had to escape, the door would be blocked, so the emergency handle on the window above would have to suffice.

I read the instructions over and over. *Pull handle out. Pull handle down. Push window out. Pull handle out. Pull handle down. Push window out. Pull handle out. Pull handle down. Push window out.*

I scan the crowd to see if any new faces took advantage of my mental lapse. No one has.

Two and a half hours later, I arrive in New York. The massive buildings and clean look of the newly built city hide the filth inside. The impenetrable two-hundred-and-fifty-foot Leviathan wall that surrounds the city sparkles in the sun. Its copper-colored body sticks out like a sore thumb. It has one entrance and exit on the far side of the city, so any coyotes trying to sneak people into the Little Villages have a long walk to escape back into Nowhere.

The view of the city disappears as the monorail pulls into the station. The automated conductor plays over the intercom its generic goodbye as the people stumble out of the monorail like a herd of cattle. They follow their designated path out of the station, never deviating from their routines. The gray stone floor and columns of the station are clean, sparkling as the sunset hits the quartz in the stone.

As I ascend from the staircase and become level to the black street, I am approached by one of the robotic police officers. Only this one is pink with a purple moon on its shoulder. It's an older model, probably from the late 2040s, but it shines like it's brand new.

Oh, G.L.E. has robots now. That's good news for all of us.

"Hello, Mr. O'Scandrick," it says in a metallic male voice, "I am Officer 19177. I am here to escort you to *The Late Show with Joe Jorgenson*." After the voice changes to the excited reading of the show's title that plays over the intro, it switches back and says, "Do you accept?"

"No," I respond, bored, "and tell Marshall and Elani to decommission you. You sound like an anthropomorphized cigarette."

The robot assesses my response. Its blank, emotionless face gives no sign of a decision.

As I wait in anticipation, a scream and the shattering of glass emanates in one of the apartments above the station. A man calls what I assume is his wife or girlfriend "a whore" and slaps her so hard I can hear the contact from the ground floor. Another smack and a massive thud follow. The robot officer leaves me and runs up.

There really is no place like home.

I walk up the staircase. The sidewalk and street above are perfectly clean. Not even a scratch on the mural in the middle of the road. There are no cars, just papers blowing in the howling wind. All the small buildings in the city look the same, tall and rectangular with a black finish. My watch reads 5:12 p.m. The show started seventeen minutes ago.

Excuse for being late one: I'm sick, so that slowed me down. True, but she'll call bullshit. Excuse two: The monorail was moving surprisingly slow. More probable than her believing I'm sick, but still, "Should have planned for that." Excuse three: Marshall sent another cop to escort me. I'll go with three.

Satisfied, I walk to the theater. Across the street is the New York Mall. Of course, the first place in the city is the gift shop. For at least a mile in each direction, shops, bars, restaurants, and theaters line the street all the way to the barrier fence that circles the city. Each have fancy lights to try and attract people into their stores. Hundreds are in the street anticipating the 5:30 public theater display that happens every Friday.

Weaving my way through the horde, I walk past a couple of restaurants and turn into the alley leading to the massive parking lot for the rebuilt Ed Sullivan Theater. The theater looks the same as the original, attached to a fake office building. The "building" is just painted on to the side of the monstrous auditorium for nostalgia's sake. The red letters of *The Late Show* shine bright in the intentionally shadowed parking lot.

As I make my way in, glass shatters behind me. Back by the station, the crowd scurries and gasps as a fat man in a tank top and shorts falls from the sky. He lands across the street, disappearing behind the crowd. The pink G.L.E. bot from the station follows him, jumping from the window he just shattered and lands with a bang. Dramatic music begins, and the crowds' hands throw up into the air as they cheer fanatically. The officer drags the fat man, unconscious and bleeding from his head, into a recently arrived white SUV. As the officer takes him away, dramatic music builds, the lights of the surrounding buildings shut off, a holographic lion roars, and the party begins.

Nice recovery.

Through the shattered window is a woman. She is half-naked, wearing sweats and a dark blue crop top. Her reddish-brown hair flows as the cold air fills her apartment. Her pale, freckled face is stained with the fresh blood flowing from her lips and nose. A handprint lies perfectly placed on her gorgeous face. It's almost like I can see the conversation going on in her head, "Should I stay with the man I thought I loved or leave to maybe find happiness?"

I smile at the woman, and she does the same. At least she's capable of doing so. I can help her. Unlike the mother and her kids, there is no barrier preventing me from getting to her.

Yes, there is. You know there is. And there is no way to beat it.

It's called depression, and it sucks. Disgusted with myself, I brace for boredom and head toward the theater, ready for whatever happens next.

CHAPTER 10

THE SHOW PART ONE

LEVI O'SCANDRICK
DECEMBER 22, 2064

The alley leading to *The Late Show* is shorter than most of the microstreets that web through the city. It still has its unique ad: A bright green holographic Spinosaurus paces up and down the walkway. On the ground below reads, "Meet Spinosaurus. Egypt's most terrifying beast! Only at the American Museum of Natural History in New York."

Great. Now we're stealing bones from them too?

The end of the microstreet reveals the football field-sized parking lot for the show and the sports arena. Cars are packed in the rows of the lot. Tigress Arena lights up the would-be dark parking lot a deep shade of orange. The chants of, "Let's go Tigers, let's go!" followed by old-timey sports area music echoes from the stadium.

On the opposite end of the lot, *The Late Show*'s glowing red letters mix with that of the orange, matching the hue of the darkened sunset above. Spotlights streak across the sky, encouraging viewers to enter the theater. *Of all the things to bring back for the apocalypse, it had to be talk shows. And not just as an afterthought, as a "primary necessity." No wonder no one knows what's really going on if things like this pass as entertainment.*

The closer I get to the theater, the quieter the lot becomes. No speakers blasting horn-based music. No annoying automated voice telling viewers where to enter and the rules of the show. No robotic security. *Why is no one here? Are they trying to surprise me? Is this how they get me to look like an idiot on TV again? If Fat Joe jumps out at me, I'm going to punch him in the nose. I'll still look like a fool, but at least I'll get something out of it.*

As I walk past the final row of cars, I approach the theater. JJ's maple-colored hands brush through his hair as he sits on the curb. Aisling vigorously paces behind him, her strides stretching out her short, tight blue dress. Kaiya plays "I Spy" with Jackson pointing to different cars parked in front of them. Joe sits on the curb, sweat beading down his chunky neck. His eyes are wild as he scans the parking lot. *Their documentary was approved by Marshall years ago. Why would he cancel it now?*

Kaiya approaches my paralyzed self, Jackson following closely behind. Her short blue hair is perfectly straight, barely grazing the tops of her shoulders. She wears her icy blue contact lenses to match her dyed hair color. Her black maternity jumpsuit hides her small baby pump. Jackson follows her in his baggy fireman jacket and blue jeans. He hugs me. I pick him up and place him in my arms.

"They canceled on us," she says, shaken. "We did everything right. I don't know why they would do this."

"What did Joe say?" I ask, scanning the blood orange lighting for any signs of electric blue eyes, "Marshall usually at least gives a reason to the public."

"'Unforeseen circumstances.' Whatever that means."

Flew too close to the sun with this one. Message received. "Hey," I command loud enough for everyone to hear, "We should really get going—"

"Oh, don't be such a drag, Levi," Joe's barreling voice interrupts, "We were just catching up. Give us a few, yeah?" He only has one volume: loud and dumb. He wraps his meaty right arm around JJ, who uncomfortably accepts it. His arms pinned to his body. Despite speaking to me, Joe still scans the parked cars.

What is he waiting for?

Aisling makes eye contact with me. Her hazel eyes wide. She wears a tight, light blue dress. With her black hair and olive skin, she looks like a fashionable robotic police officer. "You know, Joe," she approaches the host and kisses him on the cheek, "I think it's best if we leave. We'll catch up with you later. Does that sound good?"

"No," Joe says, still holding JJ tightly, "I think *now* is perfectly fine." Joe releases JJ, who takes a couple of steps away from him and straightens his black and red suit. His clean-shaven face grows a "shit grin," as Aisling would call it. One corner of his mouth grows into a smile while the other side resists, giving away his newly formed scheme. *He's got something planned for Joe.*

The Late Show's theme song blasts over the speakers sending a shock wave through my rattled body. It's deafening. Shock is replaced by a sharp pain in my skull. Jackson covers his ears with his hands and digs his face into my chest. I can't hear, but JJ pushes Joe, yelling something at him. Joe shrugs and shakes his head. He points to the theater, gesturing for JJ to follow. He holds the door open for JJ and Aisling. Before entering, he puts his hand out and yells what I assume is,

"Wait here," before disappearing behind the golden stained-glass doors.

Odd? Keep the genius engineer away from the malfunction.

A car door opens. Out steps an extremely tall, muscular man in a white mask. Two more men exit vehicles surrounding us. They're dressed identically to the first: white clothes, white mask, red falcon over the right eye. All three look the same: tall, white, and extremely muscular. With large, serrated swords in their hands, they approach.

"Kaiya!" I yell over the music. She grips my hand tightly, dragging me into the theater. We burst through the doors. The lobby is dark, the only light coming from the opened theater doors. As the doors close behind us, the sound of music muffles. "Joe!" I yell. *Is that why he was staring so intently into the parking lot? Did he sell us out? On what, though? Everything in this documentary was already approved.*

Kaiya leads us into the main part of the theater. The flashing rainbow lights of the room blur my vision. The rapid rotation of the rainbow lights makes my stomach churn. My already aching head worsens. The rows of red chairs are empty, the stage dimly lit. Standing at the blue curtain leading backstage, JJ yells, "C'mon, man! Don't make me carry you outta here!"

Glass shatters behind me. Between the doors that separate the lobby from the main stage, the men in the white masks pick small pieces of stained glass from their clothing. They laugh and high five each other as if this is fun for them.

Who are these guys?

"Hey!" Kaiya yells, "Stare later. Run now!" She yanks my arm, pulling me behind the curtain. Backstage Joe is fiddling with a painting of Stephen Colbert. His hands scramble as they push on the previous host's face, the corner of the picture frame, and anywhere else near the portrait.

"Who were those guys?" Aisling asks panting. Her tight dress rides up her legs, struggling to stay on.

"Who knows and who cares," Joe responds, wheezing. "Once I get this door open, we'll be safe."

"Oh sweet, you have a panic room!" JJ exclaims, relieved.

"Yeah … sorta." Joe presses the C of Colbert, and the wall grumbles. Behind it, a dark brick tunnel. "Safe room's at the end of the tunnel," Joe exasperates.

Heavy footsteps boom from the theater. We run down the short tunnel. A light shines bright at the end, signaling the location of the room. Joe beats everyone there. He types a code into a keypad on the thick steel door. Gas releases as the chamber opens. We follow Joe inside. He seals the door.

The safe room is dark, concrete, and circular. It's archaic decorated with cobwebs and minimal wooden furniture. Paintings of previous hosts were lined on the walls, from Ed Sullivan to Fat Joe. I take a look around. Aisling is fine. She's taken off her high heels, which had broken during the run. Her blue dress gave into the pressures of running and is torn. She rests against the concrete wall, looking between JJ and Joe. Kaiya's hands are on her knees. Jackson whines, "I want down!" I put him on the floor. He promptly runs over to his mother and hugs her.

"Hey!" fat Joe Jorgenson yells at me, "What the hell was that?" He pushes me backward, and I stumble a few feet. "You trying to get us all killed?" He pushes me again, this time with more force.

"Aye," JJ yells at Jorgenson as he pulls him back, "stop with the pushing and let's get a move on. Where the hell can we go? You led us straight into a dead end."

Kaiya holds Jackson, who hides behind her leg, clenching it for protection. His eyes are filled with tears. *Why did he have to be involved in this mess? Why my son?* Every effort now is to save his life and Kaiya's. No one else really matters. Not even me. It's time to be the hero I've always pretended to be. Jackson catches me looking at him. He's trying to put on his brave face for me. I can tell. His eyes scrunch up like the cartoon characters he watches on TV. With his face all contorted, he looks like the time he was trying to poop on the toilet for the first time. I remember him grunting and yelling that he can't do it and him throwing a fit. *I've got to save his life.*

"Here's my plan," Joe yells at JJ. "Now, will you back off! If it wasn't for your stupid documentary, I wouldn't have had to report y'all to G.L.E. What the hell's on the flash drive of yours anyway?"

He what?

"Well, it's pointless now," JJ yells back. "You knew the risks coming into this, and you literally invited them."

"Oh, don't feed me that bullshit, Jones!" Joe grumbles, "You're as full of shit as they come!"

"Joe," Aisling says forcefully. Her voice is firm yet restrained as she tries not to yell. "Please just stop yelling at us. We're all scared about what's just happened too, so please, let's just calm down." Her voice quivers by the end of her sentence. JJ walks over to Aisling and puts his arm around her. Her hazel eyes pool with water.

Flash drive? What is he talking about? Ask Kaiya later. It's me he wants. I can walk out there. End this for everyone.

Jackson can't stop hiding behind Kaiya's leg. He whimper's as he stuffs his face into his mom's dress. *At least make this easier for him.*

"Fine," Joe says still with hostility. "Listen up. I have a secret passage that can lead us out to Nowhere and …"

"Nowhere!" Kaiya yells at Joe, "We can't go to Nowhere! We don't got our masks, no weapons, and Jackson …"

"Jackson will be fine," I say, walking up to Kaiya. "He's tough as an ox, right kid."

"Yup!" Jackson says enthusiastically. "Tough as an … what's an ox?"

I smile and pat Jackson on the head. Kaiya stares at my shaking body. She knows I'm just trying to comfort the boy. She and I both understand there's a good chance if we go to Nowhere, we won't be coming back … at least in one piece. But it's our only choice.

"It's the only option we have," I say to Kaiya, though she doesn't seem convinced with the decision, "If we go back out there, we're not making it past those buffoons. Plus, the cops are undoubtedly on their way. They will interrogate us, and I'm sure we'll be convicted on some bullsh—" *No cussing in front of the kid,* "something. And you know our chances of surviving in Nowhere have to be better than in Marshall's prison."

"That's great, and all, Levi," JJ says to me, "but how are we supposed to get back in? I mean, we're as good as …" he says and pauses, looks at Jackson, "we're tryna get back to our homes, though. Right?"

"We can sneak back in with a coyote," I say quickly, hoping the idea doesn't have time to register in people's minds.

There's a brief pause before Joe starts laughing his barreling, iconic laugh. "Oh my God, we're all going to die! You want to go with the *coyotes*? They'll rather cook us over a fire and eat us than help us back into here," he yells in disbelief.

Jackson clings to Kaiya's leg, hiding from Joe.

"Levi," Aisling says, concerned, "the odds of us making it back on a coyote run are …"

"I know," I stammer, "but it's better than zero."

Why the hell is Marshall doing this? I haven't broken any rules. Doesn't matter. Stay in the moment.

We know that either way's a low chance of survival, but going back's a death trap. Even if we make it out of here alive, which we most likely won't, and make it past the interrogation, which we, or at least I, definitely won't, they'll just come for me again. Nowhere is our best option.

"As for weapons," Joe says, breaking the silence. He pulls the desk over and reveals two shotguns lying in a pit. "I think these will suffice." He tosses one to JJ and keeps the other for himself. Moving the lone table in the room, he reveals a cellar door. He scans his hand on a panel on the floor. A clicking sound, then unlocking metal from the floor. Reaching down, Joe struggles but lifts a thick steel door that reveals a tunnel beneath the floor.

Metal scrapes metal. The men from earlier bang on the safe room door, slashing it with the swords. "Ladies and the boy first," Joe says with urgency. "Let's get moving."

Wow, what a fucking gentleman.

Jackson is the first to climb down the rope ladder, followed by Kaiya, then Aisling. JJ goes next with a shotgun in hand. As I am about to drop, Joe grabs me and whispers into my ear, "Don't think you're getting off so easily. I know who he was here for." The stench of rum on his breath stings my eyes. He lets go of my arm and pushes me back. I stare at him, baffled that the fat man would know so much about me.

From the entrance to the safe room, gunshots replace the sound of running. Metal feet echo down the hallway. "Finally," Joe says, relieved, "Officers, we're in hmm …"

I put my hand over his mouth, realizing that this is Marshall's attempt to assassinate me. Stunned and unfittingly proud of my aggressiveness, I hastily whisper into his ear, "You ignorant waste of breath! You really think they came here to help us?"

Joe bites my hand. I scream and stumble backward.

"Not you, obviously. I'm making a bargain, trading your life for mine. Your family will be fine in Nowhere with those guns. But you and I are staying—" *Bang!* Before he finishes his sentence, fat Joe gets shot through his blob of a head and collapses to the ground. More bullets fly and turn the rest of his body to shreds.

CHAPTER 11

THE SHOW PART TWO

LEVI O'SCANDRICK
DECEMBER 22, 2064

I grab the shotgun and dive into the hole. Headfirst, I land and see stars. *Probably a mild concussion. Could be worse.* JJ closes and locks the latch.

Helping me up, Kaiya says, "Now I know why you hate talk shows."

I smile at the blurry two of her I am seeing, then check on the boy. "All right, little man," I say as I stumble over to Jackson. "How's my brave hero doing?"

He smiles his crooked grin and says, "Great!"

He's not registering what's going on. This is going to mess him up later in life.

"Yeah? Guess you are turning into a *real man* then, huh?"

"Really, Levi," Aisling says to me, disappointed.

"Yeah!" Jackson chuckles, curbing Aisling's pessimism.

"I'm just like the Fantastic Man!" I chuckle at his enthusiasm.

"Yeah, you are, kid. Yeah, you are."

Just remember to smile. What the hell caused all this? This flash drive ...

"Hey—" JJ rips the loosely tied rope ladder from the ceiling. It collapses an inch away from me. "We should get moving," he says, holding Aisling with his left arm and firmly clenching the shotgun in his right. "I don't know how long it'll take before the cops find their way in."

"Hopefully a while," Kaiya says. I still don't know why, but anytime she gets stressed, Kaiya's Michigan accent gets thicker when she speaks.

My vision clears as we start our walk through the tunnel. The walls are brick, trapping the cold air inside. The hard, tan dirt ground like concrete. Most of the lights that line the walls are out, making the tunnel a dark pathway. Each of us have one hand on the icy wall.

I am stunned at how well Jackson's doing. He walks next to Kaiya, holding her hand as he stumbles through the darkness. Any other kid would be screaming and crying at this point, but not Jackson. He's an O'Scandrick.

As we continue to walk, I notice Aisling's limp. She probably rolled her ankle running in her high heels. She's barefoot now, holding her heels in one hand and leaning on JJ's shoulder with the other for support.

There's a loud rumble followed by at least three heavy objects hitting the ground behind us.

"The door …" JJ says as we exchange glances of worry.

"We need to move," Aisling yells at everyone. "Now!"

We run. Aisling hobbles on her one good foot as JJ pulls her along. Kaiya picks up Jackson. I hold up the rear, making sure the bots get me before anyone else.

If I hadn't worked for the government, if I hadn't built the wall, none of this would be happening. Our Paradise Cities would be flourishing, and Nowhere would be nonexistent. Instead, I let my ego and my emotions cloud my reason. Now, my family is at risk. I should be the only one about to die, running for his life, not them. They did nothing wrong.

Then end this. If I just fall back …

The sound of metal feet intensifies. "JJ," I yell as we continue to run, "toss me your gun!"

"What?"

"Toss me the gun!"

"Hell no!" He stops running and lets Aisling, Kaiya, and Jackson pass him. They pause, but we shoo them along. They continue without us.

JJ lines up the shot and pulls the trigger. An officer's head snaps back, and his body explodes, just like how I designed them. *Guess his time at the range with Kaiya really helped his shot.* JJ fires at another, forcing me back to the situation.

"What the hell are you doing!" I yell at him. "Saving your ass, now run!"

"No, you're not. This is my fault …" I aim at an officer, but JJ shoots it before I can, "… not yours. If anyone dies, it's on me!"

"Aw c'mon, Levi," he says sarcastically as he still focuses on the remaining cops. "Why are you such a self-centered jackass? You really think they're here *just* for you?"

"What do you mean? Of course, they are! No one else here had anything to do with that—"

Down the hallway, a thunderous roar grows as more police officers trample their way toward us.

"Yeah, yeah. We can debate who should die later," JJ yells back mid-sprint, "but we gotta move."

We take off. The sound of metal footsteps grows behind us as more cops join the chase. I was trying to save his life and give him a future, but here he was, a better father to

Jackson than I ever could be. He and Aisling just got married, hadn't even lived yet. His ignorance is unbelievable.

Stupid selfless jackass.

We catch up to the girls and Jackson, who frantically try to kick down a door. Since one's crippled, the other pregnant, and the third is six years old, their efforts are failing.

"Move," JJ shouts as he runs up to the door. Pointing the gun at the knob, he pulls the trigger and blasts open the door. We barge inside. We are in a basement. The only light comes from the inside of a teal-colored pool in the center. The moisture makes the black rocks that cover the floor sleek and shiny. An old, rotting, moldy staircase is on the left.

Together, we climb. A brown door marked with a falcon lies at the top. As Aisling, Jackson, and JJ enter the other room, four bots knock down the door on the opposite side. They fire their weapons at us, unleashing a torrent of lead.

Stay behind and end this. Don't let them get hurt because…

Kaiya tackles me into the other room, barely escaping the gunfire. We roll away from the door as bullets continue to shred the wall. JJ, lying flat on his gut, army-crawls to the door and closes it. Aisling is able to push an old metal bookcase on it. Bullets smack the back of the bookcase but do not penetrate. Not even a moment later, the cops bang on the door, try to knock it down.

"Mom, I'm scared," Jackson says, crying as he pulls his mom's leg.

And there it is.

"We've got to keep moving," JJ says to us, out of breath.

"But where do we go?" Aisling asks, "I don't think we can keep running much longer."

She's right. All of us are exhausted. Aisling's ankle is swollen and purple. Jackson hangs onto his mother and refuses to let go of her. Kaiya has a cut on her chin and holds her stomach, fatigued. She looks up at the ceiling panting like a dog. Blood pours from her calf, most likely the result of a bullet. JJ's arm is bleeding. He also has a flesh wound. Nothing a few stitches won't fix, but still noteworthy.

Stop trying to die. They won't let you. I don't know whether to be touched or ticked. Take control. They need you now.

I examine the room. Well lit. A giant Persian rug on the wooden floor. A massive crystal chandelier hangs from the ceiling, filling the room with light. Two doors are on the wall on the left side of us. A ballroom, huge and empty. Two staircases lead up to the higher levels.

"Aisling," I say faintly, "I don't think running matters anymore. We'll find a place to hide in the mansion. It's definitely big enough where we can lose them in here. They're Gen 4 models. They're not wired to track, only for attacking and crowd control." I turn to JJ. His red shirt is stained, soaking in the blood. "How many bullets do you have left?"

"I don't know, man, like three. If you're tryna say we fight 'em ..."

"No. You know I'm smarter than that. We just have to make sure we can survive if they find us. But for now, let's just go."

We run up the stairs.

Three bullets?

These look to be standard-issued shotguns, so that means we should have six to ten shots. JJ shot two cops, missed one, and the door. He has six at best. I haven't fired yet, so that means I've got ten. Slim odds, but still doable if we make each shot count.

JJ hands Aisling the gun, picks her up, then proceeds to carry her up the stairs.

Getting a better look at her ankle, I can actually see it's dislocated, the bone protruding out of place underneath the skin. Holding in a gag, I continue with my family in front of me.

The rest of the mansion is not lit as well. At the top of the stairs is a living room which leads to two hallways, one on each side. A little bit of light from the hallway finds its way in, highlighting our escape routes like they do in the video games Jackson and I play. The chandelier that once hung from the ceiling is shattered on the rotting hardwood floor. Where it used to hang is a hole in the ceiling, letting in the moonlight.

Has it really been that long? We—

A loud bang emerges as the cops burst through the door. More emerge, tearing apart the wood frames like they were made of paper. One busts through the floor, grabs JJ by the ankle, and violently drags him back. JJ tosses Aisling away from him, but she is intercepted by another cop that runs up the staircase. She struggles with her bad ankle.

"JJ! Aisling!" Kaiya yells as she starts to run back to them.

"No!" I yell and grab Kaiya by the arm, "They've got a gun. They can take care of themselves. We have to run. C'mon!"

Hesitantly, Kaiya agrees and sprints down the hallway. I pick up Jackson and carry him. He puts his face into my shoulder and closes his eyes.

We have to make it out of here—for him. That's all that matters.

A gunshot echoes down the hallway as we run. JJ and Aisling scream as they fight for their lives. Two more shots. Kaiya, Jackson, and I duck into a room. Immediately, we slam the door shut. I put Jackson down and help Kaiya seal the door with a red couch.

The room is pretty large and has a fireplace on the back wall. A stuffed falcon lies on top of its white stone exterior. Behind it, a stone is missing, revealing another completely dark room behind it. Using what little light seeps through the hole, I look inside and find there are no other entrances to it.

A safe room.

I examine the fireplace for a lever, a button, or anything that can open it. More gunshots from JJ and Aisling's brawl with the cops. Kaiya grabs the shotgun and faces the door in anticipation. I try examining the fireplace again for a lever.

"It won't budge!" I yell at Kaiya.

She puts her finger over her mouth, signaling for me to stay quiet. Slowly walking over to me, she whispers, "What do you mean it won't budge? It's a door to another room! It's got to budge!"

"Ahh!" JJ yells and hits the ground with a thud so hard I can feel the vibration from where I am standing. Another thud follows. "Aisling. You ... You—" silence.

Kaiya and I freeze and stare at the door, waiting for an attack to occur. Metal footsteps clank closer to us. As they approach, their sound is accompanied by two bodies dragged behind them.

This is all my fault. If I hadn't ... If I didn't ... they ... No. I don't have time for this.

I stare at Kaiya's petrified face. Her icy blue eyes are wide and filled with fear. *They are all I have left.* The sound of footsteps fades away as the cops run past us.

"Hey," Kaiya whispers to me, "if something goes wrong ... if we don't make it out, take this. No matter what, don't give it away. No matter what." In her hand is a small gray flash drive no bigger than her pinkie finger.

What?

"Mom! Dad!" Jackson yells to us across the room. I dive over to him and put my hand over his mouth.

The sound of creaking wood echoes as more cops move past us. Jackson taps my arm vigorously. He has removed a book from the bookshelf next to the fireplace. Smart just like his old man. After the footsteps disappear down the hallway, I push a button hidden in the shelf. The fireplace turns away from us, revealing the hidden room on the other side.

We run through, Jackson, Kaiya, then me. No sound of metal footsteps follows us. No banging on the door. Either we are safe, or the bots are waiting for us on the …

Realizing the trap too slowly, the lights shut off, turning the mansion pitch black. Jackson screams, fearing the dark. Kaiya grabs my arm firmly, Jackson holds on to my leg for dear life. My brave little man has taken more than most kids probably could even imagine. He is living a nightmare. In the dark, two pairs of blue eyes appear. Seeing nothing but the tiny blue circles sends shivers down my spine.

I've failed them. That's it. We've lost.

As a family, we walk backward into the previous room, knowing it is secure. I grab the poker from the fireplace, then Kaiya regrips the shotgun and fires in the dark. The muzzle flash briefly reveals the decapitated body of one of the robotic officers. The body explodes, revealing a swarm of cops entering through a hole in the back wall.

A dim red light turns on, faintly unveils the destruction of the safe room. As we approach the entrance into the original room, Jackson cries. A bot has a hold of his leg, dragging him back into the safe room. The door seals. Diving for my son, the poker gets caught in the closing stone fireplace and snaps.

"No! Jackson!" I kick the stone fireplace violently, "Jackson!" Running over to the bookcase, I start yanking down every book on the shelf trying to find the latch for the door. Knocking over a blue book, *The Wright Way*, the button emerges, and the door begins its slow opening.

Jackson's screams fade in the distance.

Kaiya screams Jackson's name but gets no reply. She barges through the now opened fireplace, ready to kill, but the cops have evacuated the room. Following our son's screams, she runs through the shattered door to the hallway.

Bang! Bang! Bang!

I emerge on the other side, seeing a blood trail flowing down the wood hallway. The red emergency light reflects off the blood like the sun would on a river. At the end of the hallway is Jackson. He is crying in the grasp of one of the officers. The officer's blue-lit eyes stare gleefully at me as he holds a gun to my son's head.

Where's Kaiya?

The world around me seems to freeze. From me collapsing to the floor in a heap of despair to the flicker of the red light, nothing seems to be moving. Only my boy, my son, trapped because of me.

Behind me comes a cackling of someone choking. Kaiya lies on the floor coughing up blood, her white dress crimson. She turns to me. Her red hair sticks to the blood pooling around her. I try to move but can't. Grief has paralyzed me. Through my tears, Kaiya attempts to raise her hand to me. In it, the flash drive. I crawl over to her and grab the drive from her hand. Before I can say anything, her eyes glaze over. Her arm drops with a hollow thud.

My hands land in her blood. Sitting back on my heels and sobbing. My wife's blood on my hands. My heart strains as if someone's playing tug of war, turning it to dust. My breathing sporadic. The lump in my throat is so large it hurts. Stars impair my vision. My body tingles with pins and needles. I pocket the flash drive. *All for this…*

"Dad," Jackson whimpers.

I cannot move. My neck's strained, my jaw clenched. Vision blurred by tears. I'm on my hands and knees. I turn back to the robot. If they are still the same as before, Marshall is watching me, watching this like it's some TV show.

Jackson cries. The robot's gun placed on his temple. Its metal hands have torn through his firefighter jacket.

"Marshall," I croak, choking on my words. A new wave of tears floods my eyes, blurring my vision. My vocal cords strain. "I'm begging you, please stop. He had nothing to do with this. Just let the boy go. You've got me. You've already got my wife. Please, I'm all yours. But Jackson, he has nothing to do with my actions. Please, just let him go."

The robot doesn't react. Its paralyzed, emotionless face continues to stare blankly at me. His gun cocks.

"Marshall! Don't! Don't! I'm sorry for everything! For leaving you, for ruining your precious plan. You can take me, beat me in the damn street if you have to, but leave my son out of it."

Metal steps erupt behind me, but I continue to stare at my son. His eyes are shut, his face red and clenched.

"My arrogance," I say, barely able to speak. "This is what I get for it. This is what I get for hurting so many people. Whatever comes next is all on me. It's what I deserve. So punish *me*, Marshall! Me! Not him!"

The robot continues its blank stare. Then without warning, it turns and walks away, still with my son in its grasp. Jackson squirms and screams. The officer drags him off. "Marshall!" I scream as I run toward them, "Marshall!" My wails are inconsequential as the officer continues its slow walk away.

As I get within a foot of the robot, I am hit in the back of the head with a heavy object. Like a lifeless doll, I crumble to the floor. My vision goes black, the officer turns the corner, out of view. I get one last look at my son in his fireman jacket, his eyes forcefully shut, his screams muffled by the hands of the officer.

It can't be. That can't be my last image of him.

The flash drive. "Marshall! I have it!" My arms shake violently as I dig into my pocket. I push myself off the ground. Black spots cover my vision. My heart beats in my head. A blunt object smacks the back of my skull. I collapse to the ground, impaired. I barely mumble the only word that's important to me before I pass out, "Jackson."

The distant sound of a gunshot.

CHAPTER 12

THE MAN IN THE PINK FLIP-FLOPS

JANET SIMS
DECEMBER 22, 2064

"Hmm, I don't know about that. Are you sure the pollination factories are underpaying them?" I ask Kimy as I repost her story. I hold my breath as I wait for my followers' response. I get instant love from them, who pin my post to the Pixie homepage with captions like, "Ew!" "Save the Poli workers!" and, "Fuck Levi!" I shakily exhale and like the "Fuck Levi!" comment.

Another day, another save.

I put down my phone and grab my Tigress glasses, which scan my eyes and unlock. The apps flutter into my vision, floating around me in a circle. I turn left and, toward the floor, is an ad. I eye swipe up and read, "The new Tigress Brain Chip. Be ever connected to your friends and followers. Think it, and the Tigress complies."

That looks amazing!

"And then," Kimy continues to yell, "they told him to quit if he wasn't happy working for them. Can you believe that?"

Sitting on my turquoise couch, I look out of the wall-to-wall window in my second-story studio apartment overlooking the Paradise City: New York market. The neon orange sun backlights the city's skyscrapers, casting majestic shadows across Market Street below me. The "giving street" is its usual busy, with hundreds of people shopping and eating out. Today it has these projected yellow bricks painted with two giant blue ladies blowing kisses to floating butterflies, which is so much better than last week's safari jungle theme.

When's that concert start again?

A "G.L.E. Recommendation" appears in the corner of my vision, its orange smiling moon laughs. It's G.L.E.'s lifestyle guru Circe, "Hello Lady Janet," she says in her ancient Irish accent. "Based on the data provided by you the past 372 days, it's time to have some tea. Shall I open Average Joe's?"

I grab yes. Circe opens the Average Joe's Tea app. I select Chamomile and hit start. My Average Joe's coffee/tea maker beeps and makes my beverage.

"Wow, that's terrible," I say to Kimy to keep her going.

"No, ugh, Janet! You're not listening to me again!" she yells, frustrated.

Her heart-shaped hologram cake-face is all scrunched up in front of me, blocking my view of the city. She really has to ease up on the makeup.

"They are doing both!" she squeaks. "They're like, I don't know, making people work harder to make less money. I mean, I saw a guy yesterday inside the factory using his swab to move pollen from one plant to the next for twenty-two straight hours! Do you know how boring that is?"

"Your tea is ready, Lady Janet," Circe interrupts over the speakers in the studio apartment. In my red and white stylized glass kitchen, a bell dings. Behind the cappuccino machine, my cup is filled.

"Wow, that is so awful," I respond as I walk to get my cup. "What factory was it again?" I ask as I take a sip of the hot tea.

"Average Joe's," Kimy says furiously.

I choke on the sip. *It's already bought. It'll be a waste to pour it out.* "Oh yeah, they're the worst," I say quickly as I wipe the spilled tea from my face.

A knock on my door interrupts. "Oh, hold that thought, Kimy," I interrupt, "Circe?"

Two chimes later, and Circe answers over the speakers around the apartment, "Yes, Lady Janet?"

"Who's at my door?"

Two bell chimes later, Circe responds, "Marcus Finnbauker, Lady Janet. Shall I let him in?"

"Ooh, 'Lady Janet,'" Kimy taunts. "How long ago did you change her to say that?"

"What, you don't like it?"

"No, it's so you. I love it."

Marcus knocks on the door again. "Oh, before you let him in, who was he again?" I ask Circe.

Circe projects the post I made about Marcus onto my glasses. "He is the owner of Finnbauker Shanks, the meat spot at the edge of Market Street," Circe responds in her sweet, majestic voice. The post is a great picture of me standing in front of Marcus's restaurant. If the ugliest meat joint in all of PC:NY wasn't in the background, I would totally make that my profile pic.

If he's as hotheaded as I remember, I can make a good video out of this. I may even get top ten. "Another crazy, dumb Keith." Yes! "Oh, right! Let him in and record him, Circe." I put Kimy on front view, "You're so gonna love this."

Hiding her back in my glasses, Kimy's face scrunches up again as she asks, "But what about the pollination—"

"You lying whore!" Marcus screams as he slams my front door closed. He slaps the wall with his giant, meaty hand, which makes a loud pop. The red light appears in the corner of my lens.

Ha ha, this is gonna get so many views.

"I don't even use Good King cow meat in my patties!" he yells in his high-pitched voice, "I use artificial meat and beans just like everyone else. And now you got people out there believing I use communist cow meat and boycotting my restaurant!" His hands move around in wild and aggressive motions, making him look like a lunatic.

I can work with this.

"Um, what are you doing in my home? How did you find out where I live?" I try to sound as innocent as possible.

"You post so many damn pictures. It wasn't too hard to figure out," he responds in a matter-of-fact tone.

"So you're stalking me?"

"What? Of course not—"

"Because it really seems like you are, Keith."

Infuriated, Marcus slams his hand on my red glass dining room table. He aggressively storms over to me, his face an inch from mine. "You are ruining my life, my kids' lives, by spreading that lie around. People are losing jobs because of you! You can get us kicked out of the city!"

"You should've thought about them before you used those bad products."

"I didn't do it!" he screams. "Gina posted that rumor hoping it'll catch on and ruin my business so G.L.E. could spread their land."

"Who's Gina?" I ask, snickering.

"Exactly! You don't even know what you're talking about, and yet you're posting it as if you do!"

This is going to be awesome. Holding in my laugh, I continue, "Well, if it wasn't true, then you wouldn't be so mad. As a journalist …"

"A journalist?" Marcus pulls out his phone and shows me the post I made about him a couple days ago. "That is not journalism," he yells. "That is you trying to be a cut-rate model and stir the pot. You don't work for a news agency. You have a famous Pixie account. Do you even know how many lives you ruin just because you're pretty and horny boys want to see you?"

Ouch, well, that was rude. "Okay, Keith."

"Stop calling me that! I was alive when they invented that word!"

"I'm going to need you to take a deep breath and take it down," I say and make three clicks with my tongue, "three notches. I'm just trying to have a civil conversation."

"A civil conversation? You're running me out of business because you are spreading a lie! You're falling for their trap! The only civility I'll be showing you is when I see your pretty ass in court."

Gotcha.

Acting extra, I take a step back and gasp, "Excuse me? What did you just say about my ass?"

Marcus's face flushes white. "No," he stammers, "I didn't mean it like that. Don't twist my—"

"Officer of the law at the front door," Circe interrupts.

Marcus's face turns to beat red again. "You called the cops!"

No? I can work with this. Maybe a two in one?

"No! Why would I do something like that?"

"Well, who did then?" Marcus is sweating like crazy. His white tank top is almost see-through.

"Oh, God! Circe, what's he here for?"

"Domestic disturbance," Circe announces. "He is awaiting your approval for entry."

Marcus looks at me wide-eyed. "Why would you do that?" he screams, only making this so much worse, his hands waving wildly around him, nearly hitting me in the face. "You know how bad this will be for the both of us? They'll ruin us!"

"Overriding access," Circe announces, "Welcome officer 19177."

Oh no. Stay calm.

The robotic officer runs through the door. He looks different than any of the other robo cops I've seen. His rose gold metal face and icy blue eyes pause and look around my apartment. Instead of a PC:NY Badge, a purple smiling moon. Marcus's sweaty and beet-red face is an inch away from mine. His breathing is heavy. His hands are raised in the air.

"Officer, please, everything is fine. We were just having a discussion." Seeing Marcus in his aggravated state, the officer runs in between us. One of his blue eyes flicker.

"Janet," Kimy whispers, "remember what I said about G.L.E. might having their own officer."

"Officer, please! We're not even in a relationship! He was just mad about something I said about his restaurant online." A cold metal hand hits me on the face, pushing me away from Marcus. I slide across the smooth wood floor and hit my bedroom door. Kimy screams in the background. Scared, Marcus runs to the window.

The robotic officer throws my red table aside as it approaches Marcus. The table smashes the wall-to-wall window that overlooks Market Street. Cracks spread throughout the tint, creating a spider web. The auto-tint freaks out. Some parts of the window completely clear while other parts are totally dark.

"Officer, please! We were just arguing, uh talking, uh just having a talk!" Marcus is panicking. He knows. The officer grabs Marcus's wrist and spins him around. Marcus screams and pulls away. In a moment of desperation, he pushes the officer backward with too much force, and the robot hits my window, sending more cracks through it.

"Marcus, stop!" I yell. "You can't hit him!"

"I didn't! I'm sorry," Marcus squeaks, his beady eyes the size of gold balls. His hands are in the air again as he tries to plead his case. "I didn't mean to push you, sir. It just hurt when you grabbed me."

The robotic officer recovers from his fall. A metal hand cracks against the window. The rose gold uniform torn on the torso. Standing, it approaches Marcus, picks him up like he weighs nothing, and tosses him across the apartment. Hitting the window, Marcus screams as it cracks, shattering into a million tiny pieces. He's sliding out, clawing at the floor. Kimy screams for me to flee. The officer runs toward him, but Marcus falls. Loud gasps come from below as people in the street see a giant man fall two stories.

The officer prepares to jump but freezes. Its eyes shut off, leaving blank black sockets. He turns to me. In a different, more human male voice, he says, "Stay where you are. You are currently the prime suspect in the murder of Marcus Finnbauker. We'll be back for you in a moment." Pausing for a quick second, the officer stares across the street.

After a moment, red lights flash as the Friday night concert begins. A giant holographic lion lights up the darkening city.

Wait ... that was last week's concert. What is going on?

The officer jumps out of the building, and the crowd cheers his landing.

Oh God, I'm so screwed. They think I killed him. I can't believe it. I didn't kill him. Why would they think I killed him? Is he even ... I have this recorded, though. I didn't do this.

I walk to the edge of the window. Outside, the lion show goes on. People are dancing and smiling as the upbeat music blasts. The icy wind cuts through my crop top. There is no sign of Marcus, the shattered glass, or the officer.

I don't know what I'm looking for, but I continue to stare outside. There are only a few people not dancing. A small family walks past the old Rockefeller Atlas Statue. They looked panicked. Both mothers are confused as they huddle past a perv smiling at me. Then there's a young man who's in desperate need of a shower. His face is covered in muck, and his blond hair and beard have chunks of mud in them. He wears a suit jacket that is way too big for him and walks with a limp.

Must be from Nowhere. He must be one of those coyotes! Janet, you genius, you found your answer.

"Janet! Hey, Janet! Are you still there?" Kimy asks from my screen. My glasses are cracked. As Kimy speaks, her face and voice cut in and out until she disappears. I shouldn't even be considering this. Selling out an Other? Maybe he's a cannibal or one of those weird, mutated ones? If I get too close, will he eat me? Maybe if I follow him and tell the cops, then they'll treat me better.

Walking on the yellow-painted street, the coyote takes off his soaked and destroyed shoes and tosses them into a trash bin. They vaporize inside. The blond man steals a pair of pink flip-flops too small for his feet from a rack outside a shop. He walks into an alley that has an astronaut holding a red balloon floating on the wall.

Metal footsteps echo down the hall outside the front door. It's now or never. "Circe, stop recording."

Two bell chimes later, Circe responds, "Recording stopped. Would you like to save?"

"Yes! Of course! But, Circe, I need to get out of here."

"Sorry, Lady Janet. Recording could not be saved," she answers.

"What happ—"

"You shouldn't leave," Circe says calmly. "Leaving will only make things worse. Trust the police, Lady Janet. I called them to help you. They *will* help you."

What? Crap, why would she do that?

Taking off my Tigress glasses, I quickly put on a jacket and shoes. Followed by the sound of metal footsteps, I race out of my apartment.

Hopefully, this man in the pink flip-flops will be what I need him to be.

CHAPTER 13

CITY OF BLINDING TRASH

JANET SIMS
DECEMBER 22, 2064

I peek out my door to see my empty hallway. There's no sign of the G.L.E. police. The announcement board paints the white hallway orange as ads about the new Tigress Glass Skin flash on the screen. Other than what's on the projection, nothing moves. I pull my hood over my head and gingerly walk out of my apartment. My feet echo in the empty hallway.

Oh God, why am I doing this? I can't do this. This is ridiculous. I'm sure Circe has the video hidden somewhere, and the officers record what they see. Yeah, I can fight this. I don't have to run. Butterflies fill my stomach.

I can call my parents. They can help me.

Circe's two bell chimes play in the hallway. The holographic display changes to Circe's smiling orange moon. The moon's mouth moves as she speaks in her default So Cal accent, "Pardon the interruption. Your daily programming will continue after this quick message from the Paradise City:

New York Police Department. A suspect in a murder case has decided to flee the scene of the crime in your district. Please be aware of your surroundings."

A picture of me appears, taken only seconds ago. I am walking down the hallway wearing my neon orange hoodie and sweats.

Circe continues, "Suspect Janet Sims may be found near her home on 1257 Market Street, apartment 21, near her parents' home on 902 Philadelphia Ave, or with our other suspect, Kimberly Thomas, who lives at 415 San Francisco Boulevard. If you see this woman, please ask Circe to call 911. We thank you for your time. Here's to the Good Life!"

Ugh, they got Kimy too? And now I can't go anywhere else. They're gonna find me one way or another. Do I even have a choice?

The reemerging echo of metal footsteps. Down at the opposite end of the hallway, something climbs the stairs. Fast.

Keep cool, Janet. It could be anyone. It doesn't mean that they're cops.

I turn and casually walk to the other end of the hallway.

As the footsteps get louder, I move faster. My legs work against my brain, and my casual walk quickly turns to a sprint. As the door opens on the opposite end of the hallway, I exit, running faster than I ever have in my life.

Hopping down the staircase, I quickly reach the exit. A person walks out before me. Our automated door man, Sami, doesn't say a word to him as he opens the door. When I approach, he speaks, "Hello, Lady Janet! Isn't it a wonderful day we are having?" Usually I enjoy my five-second conversations with the robot, but today …

I burst through the door to Market Street. Sami says, "I'll recalibrate for next time. Good day," I pull my hoodie over my head. There is no sign of Marcus or even a fight. My apartment is now covered with flames as the holographic lion fights fireballs. The DJ, Doobie Schitt, hovers in front of the apartments on his clear stage. Hundreds of people dance around in the street as music blasts, completely oblivious to what's going on.

Covering my face, I fast-walk onto the yellow street. The road lights up underneath my feet, which definitely helps me stay incognito. The mob of people continues to dance around me as I try to push through them. A man shoves me and yells, "Watch where you're going!" and another splashes his drink on me. More people seem to knock me around, angry cuz I'm screwing up their fun.

As drinks continue to splash, the once pleasant two-bell chimes of Circe interrupt the show. My body shivers. People boo and throw their cups at the now frozen red lion and frozen DJ. After a moment, all the holograms disappear, which brings on more boos. Circe's orange announcement box replaces it.

My picture and Kimy's are side by side. Mine's updated. I am walking out of the stairwell, staring directly into the camera with wild eyes as I pull my hood over my head. Much like mine, Kimy's pic must have been taken recently. She's next to an Average Joe's factory wearing her raggedy denim jacket. Behind her, two men in rose gold uniforms hop over a car as they chase her.

Circe turns into the G.L.E. moon and announces in her calm voice, "Sorry to interrupt your show. It will proceed momentarily. The Paradise City: New York Police Department is currently looking for two suspects in a murder investigation. Janet Sims and Kimberly Thomas. Consider them to be dangerous. Do not panic if you see either suspect. Instead, just use Circe to call 911! Thank you for your time. Here's to the Good Life!"

Circe's announcement disappears as the lion and music start up again.

Dangerous? Me? Are they joking? What the hell is going on?

Most go back to dancing to the music. However, a few creep around. A couple of people make eye contact and pull out their phones or tap their glasses. Wide-eyed, I run out of the crowd, trying to find the astronaut with a red balloon. Looking over the street, there are koi fish swimming around in white water, a dinosaur climbing a wall promoting a new movie, and a beach front ad for beer. But there's no astronaut.

Where'd it go? Did they change them already?

Spinning around, I find more people in the crowd staring at me. They look confused, trying to figure out if I'm the woman in the picture or not.

Deciding not to take a chance, I run through the nearest alley. The floor is white. Pinkish white and orange koi fish swim around me. Some jump out of the digital water as holograms, but I sprint through them. No matter how fast I dart through the ad, the fish keep following me. Finally, at the end of the alley, they stop. On the floor are the words, "Brought to you by The Dome."

Crap, where'd that Other go? He couldn't've gotten that far.

Behind me, a deep voice yells, "Freeze! If you don't, we will shoot!" An undercover police officer, this one's a human (*I thought they were banned*), is wearing a bright, flowery jump suit. His hair is all frazzled like he's been banging his head for hours. His hands shake as he holds up his badge. The koi fish swim toward him. He mumbles something into his radio, and the koi display disappears.

The alley is dark without the lit-up street. With the lights gone, there is nothing to hide how disgusting the alley is. There's trash everywhere. Litter lines the hologram panels, reaching about three feet high.

How have I never noticed this before?

"Ms. Sims," an officer grumbles, his hand heavy on his pistol, "I am asking you to stop running. All we want to do is ask you some questions."

With the light gone, all I can see of the officer is his silhouette. "I didn't do it!" I beg, "Please! You have to believe me! It was the robotic officer. He freaked out and attacked Marcus!"

"That's enough, Ms. Sims. I need you to lie face down and put your hands behind your back." He slowly approaches me, gun still drawn. He doesn't sound like a typical PC resident. His accent, it's almost Chinese …

Just because he's Chinese doesn't mean he's one of them.

"Officer, please, believe me! I didn't do it," my voice chokes over the sob I'm holding back, "I have a video of the whole thing! I can—"

"You have to the count of three," he responds. He is walking toward me slowly, with his gun still pointed at my head.

"Please, I didn't—"

"One," he says, now within one hundred feet of me. "Two," he yells before I can plead my case. Taking a few steps back, I wipe a tear away from my eye. *I have the video. That's all I need.* As I'm about to take a knee, the officer yells something. Black smoke puffs around him, engulfing the officer in a cloud. A bullet flies past my head, hitting the wall.

He shot at me! Oh dammit! I get up and run down another alley. Tears flood my eyes. Behind me, more shots are fired. *Why won't they just listen to me? They're making me give up my life all because they won't listen.* My soaked orange hoodie clings to my skin. My hair slaps me in the face. My feet blister. *I can't do this. I can't escape this place. They're gonna find me and kill me.* Turning another corner, I find another pile of trash. I take off my jacket, sit on the hoodie. Crying, I hide in it.

Goddammit, stop crying, me. Just for one second.

Ahead is Main Street. Cars fly past the end of the alleyway. Beyond that is The Dome. I've never been able to afford to go inside, but even from out here, it looks amazing. The quadrant facing me is the redwood forest. Although the glass isn't completely clear, some of the trees are visible.

Labored breathing and heavy footsteps approach. Wiping away my tears, I try holding back my sobs. Hand over my mouth, eyes closed, waiting for the officer to find me.

Scuffling footsteps get louder. They are joined by metal ones. Through a gap in the trash pile, a couple of humans in rose gold uniforms are accompanied by robots of the same coloring. All have the G.L.E. logo on their arms.

"Behind you!" the human officer yells. *What?* A loud explosion shakes the trash around me. A shot fired. Silence.

What the hell just happened?

I push the trash bag off my head. My eyes slowly adjust to the light. The body of the metal officer is scattered throughout the alley. The human officer is knocked out. A pink flip flop rests next to his face.

Wait ... is he ...

The Other from before now stands at the edge of the alley facing Main Street. His feet are bare. He looks even rougher in person. His hair is a messy nest, and his clothes are in tatters. He is bleeding from his arm, and his suit jacket is wrapped around his torso. His white shirt underneath is stained a dark red. He intensely stares at the road, then back to his watch. He sprints into the street.

Is he crazy?

But no cars come near him. Running to the middle of the road, he removes a sewage cap and jumps into the hole.

What the? Where's he going?

Jumping up from the trash, I run over to the alley. I remove my grotesque orange hoodie and toss it with the rest of the trash. Cars speed past me as I stare at the hole. It's only four lanes over, but there's no way I can reach it. Above the Dome, Circe's wanted poster pops up with a picture of me standing in the alley, looking directly at the camera. I look like crap. My white crop top is stained with some yellow sludge, and my hair is a frizzy mess. I'm starting to look like the guy I'm chasing.

The automated cars whiz past me at seventy miles per hour. They follow each other in rows, their drivers sleeping or watching some show. The cars are going the exact same speed as the one next to it. They pass me in rows. A pattern. As soon as the next row of automated cars passes me, I jump into the road.

Oh, please don't die. Worst way to go ever. Before I even get three steps in, the next wave of cars is on me. I dive back into the alley. *How did he do this?* I stand back up. Another group of cars passes me. Then another. And another. And another.

C'mon next group. Next group, do it.

The next group passes me. I take one step forward before my body says no. I stumble backward, only for a car to miss me by an inch. Sirens of police cars cry out with their flashers on as they come around the far side of the Dome. Three cops … no unmarked undercover cop cars cut into traffic, breaking the formation.

Thank you!

Running as fast I can, I dive down the sewage pipe.

CHAPTER 14

GOOD DOME

JANET SIMS
DECEMBER 22, 2064

Diving headfirst down a sewage pipe. In the blink of a second, while I am in the air, I have time to think: I should have gone feet first. I try to scramble but fail as I crash into the shiny white floor ... my arms too weak to protect my face.

The perfectly clean white floor slams into my face, sending a jolt through my body. I lie frazzled on the ground. The bump I have on my chin throbs.

My vision is still blurry, but it doesn't look like I'm being followed.

As my head clears, I look around. The tunnel is really clean, and it looks almost exactly like the all-white hallway in my apartment building. On the floor, muddy footprints run down the center.

Gotcha. This guy better be worth it.

Above me, the sewer hole light gets blocked out by what must be police cars. They are stopped, and I hear doors opening and closing. The cars take out the sunlight from outside, leaving me with only the dim lights in the hallway. I stand. My legs wobble and shake like some of the gelatin dinners I hear the poor people eat.

Should I just stop? These cops are everywhere, and this Other is nowhere in sight. Maybe I can just tell them I'm chasing an Other who is trespassing and a murderer. That may work. Heavy boots echo on the concrete above me. There's probably, like, twenty of them. *What am I thinking? There's no way they'll listen. They will kill us both.*

A cold breeze sends goosebumps up my entire body as I chase after the Other. I turn a corner before the officers enter the tunnel. Metal clanks behind me as multiple officers must be chasing after me, probably following the same footprints I am.

When I turn again, the white floor changes to dirt. Some loose roots dangle from the ceiling like all-natural chandeliers. As the light in the tunnel darkens, so do the Other's dirty footprints. Soon, they completely disappear, blending in with the dirt.

Dammit! Where'd ... which way did he go?

In front of me, a crossroad. The right has *The Dome: California Redwood Forrest* written on the side. The left has giant pipes lining the ceiling and walls.

The officers are closing in. In the distance, ten of them emerge. Some whip out their guns, and others just charge, fists raised. These aren't cops. They don't have a PC:NY uniform. They're human, wearing a rose gold uniform with the G.L.E. logo. All of them are Chinese. I try to run, but my tired legs collapse to the ground.

No, no. Not like this. Please, not like this.

Tears cloud my vision. I crawl through the muck, wheezing as I drag myself away. I beg them, barely able to say, "It wasn't me! Please! You have to listen! I didn't do it! I have proof!"

They don't even slow down. The closest leaps in the air about to hit me but freezes midflight. A dart sticks from her neck. She collapses on the ground, smacking her head on a wall.

Much like the "better days shot" I had at last New Year's Eve, a second wave of energy shoots through my body. I quickly jump to my feet and run away. Ahead of me, a tall black man with blond hair, a bloody white shirt, and a gray sport coat wrapped around him like a bandage. His hazel eyes study me. "Hi," he says in his childish voice. *What?*

"You!" one of the Chinese men behind me yell, "Come with us or die!"

"I think they're talking to you," the Other says to me. *This is it. Just say you were chasing him.*

"And you, Other," a woman in the rose gold uniforms yells, "You're not getting out of here alive."

"Oh," he complains disappointed, "I don't want to get involved in this squabble. This is her thing. Not mine."

The soldiers raise their guns. "Well, that's just rude," he says, tapping a tube on his backpack. A small black sphere falls into his hand. He tosses it onto the ground. Black smoke erupts from the sphere.

"It's poison!" yells one of the soldiers.

I dive away from the Other. Who the hell uses poison? That's so cruel! Was the dart ... Who gives a shit! Run! Picking myself back off the ground, I bolt toward the right tunnel and hide around the corner. *What am I supposed to do now? He was my only shot at things going back to normal.*

What if he can help me?

I look back over the fight. A couple of rose gold bodies lie on the floor. The Other jumps through the air, kicking one of the soldiers so hard he smashes into the tunnel wall. *Or maybe* he's one of those cannibals. Didn't Kimy tell me all these Others are cannibals? Yeah, I'm not risking it.

I take off down the tunnel. There's got to be a way out of this place. Maybe—

Rapid footsteps approach from behind. Turning around, the Other sprints directly at me. *Oh God, he's gonna eat me!* The moist dirt below is slippery, making it hard for my wobbly legs to keep me up. I can't even get into a full sprint before he tackles me to the floor. I kick and scream but can't break his grip. Death by robot sounds way better than being someone's dinner. I try kicking him in the nuts, but he has my legs pinned down.

"Help!" I scream as I try scratching his face. "Help! Anyone please he—" He puts his hand around my throat. Grip strong and ruthless. Tightening. My eyes bug out. My breathing labored. He points his gun at my face. "No," I whimper, "please. Don't eat me." His deep brown wild eyes stare directly into mine. My legs continue to kick and squirm, but nothing changes. Black spots cover the world around me. Blood floods my ears, causing them to ring.

No! Please no! I don't wanna die. I don't deserve to.

As the choking becomes unbearable and my eyes can barely see anything but black, he releases his grip. I gasp for air and wheeze. Coughing, I roll over to my stomach and slowly crawl. Although I can barely see, my arms and legs seem to move on their own. As the black spots disappear, my crawl has taken me to a wall. My neck throbs.

I've gotta get out of here. I try to stand, but my body rejects my movements. Despite his hand being gone, I still feel his grip around my neck. The cannibal sits hunched over, his gun within reach. "I'm sorry," he says calmly, "I didn't mean to take it that far. I can't do that. Even to one of you. So, uh, can you please stop chasing me, okay? It's not helping me escape. And sorry for uh ... you know," he says putting his hands around his neck as if choking himself.

Breathing is still hard. My throat seems to be broken if that's even possible. He doesn't seem to notice me. He just stares at his watch. His gun sits pretty close. I can still get out of this. I crawl toward the gun. As he speaks, his voice seems to fade away as my nerves grow.

Oh man, I can't ki—. No, don't say it. Just do it. Don't say it. Just do it ... It's just a game. Not real life. It's all fake.

"But maybe your robot buddies can help you get better," he says as he looks at his orange watch. His brow furrows. "Or they'll just arrest you or something ... you know, you're not really what I imagined for a PC person. I always thought you'd be ... I don't know. Cleaner?"

Gun in hand, I pull the trigger, but no bullets fly out. An empty click. He smirks at my mistake. *What no? No, no, no. Oh shit! Is he gonna ...* He just laughs and fiddles with his watch. He keeps smacking it and frowning. "Wow," he exasperates, "that was ... wow."

I stare at the gun and toss it to the side. "Well shit," I wheeze. "Yeah, I know," he says, laughing. "That was pretty funny. Charlie was right. You guys will take any chance to kill us." He stands up and dusts himself off. "I hope your robot buddies find you soon. It's kinda chilly in here." He takes off running down the tunnel.

"Robot buddies"?

I look back at the remains of the cops behind me. More dead cops with me while I'm being hunted for murder? I'll take my chances with the Other who won't kill me. Please don't be a cannibal.

"Hey," I barely croak out. My throat scratches. He doesn't stop running. A couple of hundred feet away, he pauses, then turns left. "Hey," I yell one more time. My throat's on fire, and my head still throbs. Stumbling to my feet, I chase after him. I can barely run in a straight line. Each breath I take is like I'm drinking boiling vodka. "Hey, come back. I'm not one of them," I try yelling. Although my voice is clearing up, it still sounds weak.

Stumbling and wheezing around the corner, I almost run into a massive root dangling from the ceiling. But as I try to dodge it, I slip on the wet ground and fall into another root. This part of these crappy tunnels is filled with these giant roots sticking out of every direction. Some dangle from the ceiling and touch the ground, making giant natural pillars.

Why can't he just stand still!

Climbing through the thick roots is like climbing through a jungle gym. The roots wrap around each other, creating a thick and really slimy maze. The farther in I go, the less light. The roots create shadows, a perfect place for the cannibal to kill me. Right, he won't. Maybe I can take advantage of that.

At the end of the maze, the Other hides behind a large drape of roots. He peeks his head into an open road in front of him. As a Jeep rolls by, he taps his backpack again and grabs another bomb. It hits the Jeep and explodes on contact. The metal head of an officer rolls to my feet.

"Dammit, Jesus," he mumbles under his breath. "Why can't you put the grenades in the left pipe like a normal person?"

Jesus?

Just be calm and assertive. I got this. He doesn't know I'm also wanted for murder. So just act like I got nothing to lose. Yeah. I can do that.

"Listen, okay? I'm not one of these ... *things*," I say, kicking the head of the exploded officer. The Other doesn't even flinch as I approach.

He smirks his childish grin as he pulls out some pointy rubber tools and fidgets with the robot's hand. "Well, duh," he says without looking up from his work. "You're something much worse than that."

"What are you insinuating?"

The other contorts his face. He asks, "What am I what?"

Wow. They really are dumb. "Ugh, no. What are you *implying*?"

He stops working on the robot's hand. Blank stare. "Implying? Really? You don't know that word. Okay. Great. I'm trying to reason with an idiot."

"Wait, what? I know what *that* means."

"I know, I know, I know," I say to calm him down, "I'm just saying ..."

His face goes from confused to angry, then back to confused.

Really? At least pay some attention to me.

"You know what?" I continue, "Never mind. Let's just get out of here. Okay?"

"Let's?" he says like the idea's ridiculous to him. "Why let's ... as in us ... no."

A piece of armor falls off the robot's hand, revealing a key inside his palm. The Other grabs the key and walks to a ladder across the street. "Oh, because if you don't take me with you," I yell at him from the other side of the road, "I'll alert every cop in the city where you are, and you'll be dead before you can even reach the wall."

Before he inserts the key into the scanner, he freezes. Turning around, his face is strained. His eyes are angry. "But they'll get you too. And by the looks of it, they really want to get you. And not to mention how bad you are at sneaking."

"I'm not bad at sneaking!"

"I heard you breathing from the other side of the tunnel," he says bluntly.

"Well, I had a little trouble breathing earlier because someone decided to choke me to death."

"I said I was sorry!"

The ground beneath the road rumbles. To our right, headlights fill the dark tunnel. The Other looks at his watch with wide eyes. He slaps it repeatedly. "We're running out of time," I pressure him. I walk into the middle of the road and spread out my arms to make sure the police see me.

"What're you doing?" he says, shaking.

"Well, unlike you, I'm a citizen. All I have to do is say you kidnapped me, and you were gonna eat me because you're a cannibal."

"What?" he yells.

"And then say you made me do all these bad things because you hurt me. And," I point to my neck, "I have the marks to prove it."

His eyes stare at the floor in disappointment … maybe he is mad that he didn't kill me.

The car engine grows louder. "Okay. Up, up. It's time to go," he says. I run over to him. He scans the card, and a latch opens in the ceiling.

"And just so we're clear," I say as I climb the ladder ahead of him, "you're not a cannibal, right?"

"What if I am? You're what? A dinner and a half." He pauses and smiles. "You are brainwashed. All of you are brainwashed," he says, looking away from me.

"Okay, jeez, sorry, I'm not brainwashed, but I just had to make sure."

The Other closes the hatch behind us. We stand in a parking garage. Lined up next to us are rows of ... things. They kind of look like cars, but they don't have doors or a trunk or seat belts or even windows. They're all rusted and look like they've been dunked in acid.

The Other walks over to one that's bright red and has what looks like "The Dome" painted on its front, but the "the" has been scratched out and replaced with "Good."

How clever.

"Are you coming or not?" the only noncannibalistic Other asks. He seems to be more fidgety than before. His eyes look around the room, and his leg shakes nervously in the driver's seat. I walk over to him and sit on the passenger side. Closer up, sweat drips down his face. His bloodied shirt clings to his body and drips onto his torn gray pants.

After a moment of sitting in silence, I ask, "Are you gonna drive?"

"Yeah, totally." He doesn't move.

"Are we waiting for something?"

"No," he whimpers. Still no movement.

"Then what is it?"

"I kinda sorta have this watch that tells me when I need to move and not move, and now that's broken, so now I'm kinda just winging it, and I'm not sure if I follow the rules exactly that I'll make it out of here fine. But Charlie says the watch is more important than the rules, or was it the other way around? And now I have you, and you're brainwashed and definitely confirming every bad thing I heard about people from here, so I'm kinda trying to remember the rhyme that deals with this."

"Wow," I respond. "That was ... a lot."

At the other side of the garage, a wall opens. As the light pours in, I get my first glimpse into Nowhere. It's as bad as people say. The white and gray ashy ground clouds the air as large white cars with red falcons painted on their doors drive inside the garage. Before I realize what's happening, the Other starts the tiny car thing and floors it. My head smacks against the hard plastic seat. With his eyes wide, the Other drives past the last white truck into Nowhere. He says, "Hit the floor and through the door," and smiles. The garage closes behind us. No one follows.

Together, we burst into laughter. Even though I'm now in a literal hell, my shoulders relax. My entire body feels like goo as I slump into the seat laughing in disbelief.

I can't believe I actually did this!

Turning around, the wall glistens orange, reflecting the setting sun. The farther we drive away, the more the knots that turned in my stomach unravel. I can't believe I did this. I just left my entire life behind with a guy who can kill me in an instant, may or may not eat me, or feed me to some Others.

"When do you think I can go back?" I ask solemnly.

"What do you mean?" he asks, wiping some dust from his eyes.

"I mean, like go back, like back to my home." His joyful eyes soften. My face must tell the whole story.

"Oh, uh, I don't really know how to say this, but that's probably not possible." He whispers.

"What, why? You're a coyote, aren't you? You can, you know, get us back in there using your ... coyote abilities."

"Um, well, since I accidentally destroyed the only tunnel to get back into here and, uh, I don't think I have any 'coyote abilities,' I probably can't get you back in for a while, miss."

"Don't call me 'miss.' I'm not your mother."

"Oh, sorry. I don't mean to anger you—"

"How old are you?"

"Nineteen. You?"

"Great. I'm getting led to my death by a nineteen-year-old, who's probably going to let us get eaten by cannibals."

The man laughs cheerfully as if cannibalism is somehow funny to him. "I told you, you're more snack size. You're barely worth the preparation time, and we would need to fatten you up before we cook you. What do you think you would taste best with? I'm kind of thinking a sausage," he mocks.

"There are cannibals out here! Everybody knows that! And now I left everyone behind at home. Even worse, I'm going to die out here and get eaten by some freaking wild beast or some savage."

The Other's face contorts as he tries his best to hold in a laugh.

"What?" I scream.

"I've lived here all my life, and I've never heard of any cannibals," he says calmly, "Don't worry. The place I'm taking you to is beautiful. Way better than that city. It's right on the Lehigh River and everything. Once I get you to Charlie, he'll happily let you stay with us. I think. I don't know. He kinda hates people from the PC's."

My face must still be teary because he quickly follows with a very unconvincing, "I'm joking. Yeah, definitely know he'll take you in."

I can't believe I did this. This is the worst day of my life.

Although I try to hold back tears, they flow anyway.

"You wanna hear a knock-knock joke?" the Other says as he awkwardly tries to pat my shoulder.

"No, what am I, five?" I scold and swat away his hand. His eyes get all wide and sad. His face blushes. I turn around and take in the Paradise City. From the outside, the city looks out of place. Light from the setting sun bounces off the wall, creating a halo around the city like a spotlight in this colorless wasteland.

Please tell me I made the right choice.

CHAPTER 15

DREAMS ARE LIES WITH SUGAR

—

ARIANNA MORALES
DECEMBER 22, 2064

The chilly Indianapolis air ruffles my hair as I stand outside my front door. The rustic door laughs at me, knowing that it's my gate to Hell.

What have we become?

A G.L.E. notification jolts me out of my trance. Pulling out my phone, the bright screen lit up by the pink moon reads, "Taxes Due: 11:59 p.m."

It's like another punch in the gut. My heart strains as I enter my home.

"Mom!" Mark yells as he runs to me. He's dressed for winter in his massive fleece coat and a blue scarf. He grabs my wrist, pulling me to my bedroom. All the windows in the house are open, there are no screens. So, the dead and dying Autumn leaves trespass through them.

Please be dead.

He's not. Lying sprawled out on my bed, Patrick is passed out. Some pills are spilled on his bare chest. He lies only in his underwear.

"I tried waking him up," Mark pleads, "but he just won't. I don't know what to do."

"We really can't do anything," I say, holding back my tears, "This is just how your dad gets when they push him too hard." Mark stares at his father with his eyes bugged out. *He shouldn't have to see this. We could've done so much better ...*

"Come on, *mijo*." I put my hand on his shoulder. "Let's leave him be." Steering him out of the bedroom, Mark quietly closes the door behind us.

As we head back toward the kitchen, he whispers to me, "Why can't you take some of the pressure off of him?"

Not this again. "I am Mark," I say, matching his quiet and reserved tone, "There's not much more we can do—"

"Don't say that!" he yells back.

Silence consumes the room. I don't know what else I can say to please him. He's getting worse with each day. He's becoming his dad.

"Mark," I say softly, "I don't think this is exactly what your father and I had in mind when we moved here. This was supposed to be our dream, but ..." I can't even finish the sentence.

He just looks down and goes to his room. I do the same. Patrick still hasn't moved. His "not" opium pills lie scattered all over the bed. His petite frame sinks into the broken mattress.

"You can always leave," Sergeant Clarke's voice rings through my head. I reach into my pollination factory uniform and grab the note. *Tomorrow: 9 a.m. Gate Z8.*

Is it worth it?

I remember the first day we moved here. Mark, Patrick, and I stand in Sergeant Clarke's office at the Center of Citizenship Affairs in Paradise City: Indianapolis. The anticipation for our citizenship announcement boils in my stomach.

Please let us in.

"We just need your signature," Sergeant Clarke's barreling voice orders. We are now in his office. He's holding out a pen for me to sign the document, agreeing to comply with the terms of the city.

I grab the pen from the Sergeant and sign my name. Patrick and Mark do the same. Mark's smile is so wide that when the sergeant sees it, he can't help but smile too.

After we all sign, a blue smiling moon appears and announces in a fun, squeaky voice, "Congratulations! You are now citizens of Paradise City: Indianapolis! Based on your questionnaire, Arianna Morales and Patrick Morales, you are both qualified for work at the Riley Pollination Factory. You will start there at 5:30 a.m. tomorrow. Talk more with Sergeant Clarke about housing and pay. We are so excited to have you with us! Here's to the Good Life!" The moon vanishes, and so does my vision.

I can't help but strain my entire body to hold back my tears. I was happy. Optimistic that our future, that this city, would be the solution to our problems. We ran away in the hopes of finding this good life. Now, looking over our molding shack we call home, with its mossy walls, leaves on the floor, and the sharp, icy air, these memories almost seem like a cruel joke. Only seven years later, and now we are being forced out. I take one last look at the glow of the inner circle of the city. Behind the apartments that don't even have windows that face us, it's like we're behind our own wall.

I wonder if they even know we're here.

I place the sergeant's note on my nightstand and collapse on my bed, next to my drugged-up husband, hoping tomorrow brings a better dream.

***

I wake up to Mark shaking me violently. "He's gone!" Mark yells.

Rolling over, I have to force my heavy eyelids open, "What?"

"Dad! He just up and anteed mumbling about some gate."

No. He wouldn't.

I jump out of bed and run straight for the door. Mark follows closely. "Where are we going?" he asks.

"Your dad might be in some serious trouble."

"What? Why?"

"I'll explain when we get there."

The Autumn day sun warms my frozen skin. The car is icy cold, but I jump in anyway. Mark rides shotgun and buckles in. Starting the car, I speed to the gate. It's only a couple of minutes away driving normally, so speeding should shorten the time.

When we arrive, we're too late. Patrick yells at the officers at the gate, flaunting the note for everyone to see.

"What's dad doing here?" Mark asks with his voice shaking.

He can't ruin this for us too. Not this time. I get out of the car and run to Patrick.

"Mom!" Mark's muffled voice yells.

One of the officers is obviously flustered by the random druggie babbling to him about a meaningless note. He puts his hand on his gun as my husband's voice and body language get more aggressive. This is when I wish I voted for those robotic police officers to be used in this city. At least they wouldn't be so easily flustered.

"What do you mean, 'No?'" my husband shouts, "*La nota.*" Patrick aggressively shakes the note an inch from the officer's face, "says come here at nine. It's nine! *Que esta pasando?* What's going on!" As he yells, Patrick spits in the officer's face. With his glassy eyes and skin and bone frame, he looks like some of the Others who've snuck into the city.

"I need some ID," the officer says aggressively.

"My ID? I've lived here for seven years, and you want some ID?"

"Sir, please calm your tone and tell me your ID number."

As I'm about to reach my husband, he spits in the officer's face. *No.*

The officer immediately tackles Patrick to the broken concrete road. He slams his knee into Patrick's head. Within a second, there are four more officers on the scene. One looks at me with wild eyes. It's Sergeant Clarke. As he makes the connection, he orders an officer to replace him as an unnecessary weight to pin my husband down.

He approaches me, gun drawn. *What's he doing?*

"Do you know this man?" he asks in his extra deep cop voice.

"What?" I respond confused, "Of cour—"

"Do you know this man?" He interrupts.

Another officer approaches, gun drawn. "Dave you—"

"I know this scene is chaotic, ma'am," he interrupts again, "but for your sake, I hope you do not know the man who assaulted an officer."

The rest of the officers are now focused on us. Patrick is out cold, cuffed on the ground. "Ma'am!" he yells again, "Do you know this man who just assaulted one of our officers? For your sake, I hope not."

Is he signaling something to me?

Dave shakes his head.

He wants me to leave Patrick behind? I … I look at Patrick cuffed on the ground. Footsteps approach from behind me. Mark is running toward us with a wild look in his eye.

I'm sorry.

"I do not. I want to leave this city," I say to the Sergeant.

A slight grin slides onto his face. As fast as it appears, it's gone, replaced by his angry cop face. "As you wish," he says. Grabbing me, he walks me over to the gate.

"Hey!" Mark yells, "What the hell are you doing with my—"

"Are you related to this woman?" David interrupts. "What? Yeah, that's my mom. But—"

"Great!" David interrupts, "Then you're out of here, as well."

"What? Hey!" Another officer grabs Mark as he kicks and resists.

The metal gate creaks open slowly. As Mark continues his screams, David yells over him to prevent Mark from being heard. Mark gets one final push before being thrown on the other side of the gate. He lands face-first into the dry, grassy field. I follow him, landing hard on my side.

The outside air is dry, scratching my throat with each breath. Nowhere must really be as bad as they say. The dirt is as solid as concrete. The few remaining trees are dry brittle. Ancient-looking houses cover the outside area as far as the eye can see.

Do people still live in them? What are they going to do when they see us?

Guns cock behind us as we stand. Sergeant Clarke looks at us, rifle pointed, and says, "Congratulations! You are no longer welcome into the great Paradise City of Indianapolis. Good luck with your lives out there! You'll need it!"

Through the fence, I can see his bottom lip quiver. Only if the rest of the people in this world were as nice as him.

"This is bullshit!" Mark yells back. He looks at me, his eyes wide with confusion and fury. I can't even look at him.

"Calm down, *mijo*—"

"Don't call me that!"

"Permission to shoot, sir?" an officer asks.

"Denied," David responds, "Close the gate!"

The large gate creaks as it slowly descends, blocking us from our old lives. Before it can even close, Mark runs at it. He tries sliding underneath the gate, but it closes before he can reach it. His body slams into it with a hollow thud. The glassy gate's tint emerges, blocking our view of Paradise City.

The dry, gray, grassy neighborhood is barren. Nowhere is truly colorless.

"Running away sounds great in the beginning, but when you get out there, beyond that wall, you realize… it's all just the same. Same struggles, same fight, just a different location," Sergeant Clarke's voice echoes in my head.

I can't believe my life is as good as it gets. This dream will be better than the last.

CHAPTER 16

DO ALL DAYS START THIS BAD?

—

JAVIER JONES
DECEMBER 23, 2064

From complete black, light now blinds my eyes. Painfully squinting, waves tumble and crash in the distance. Blurry, I think I'm on a beach. There's a blueish, gray sky. The golden sand burns my bare feet. The green and blue water splashes no more than a hundred yards away. I'm alone. To my left, nothing but sand, dark sky, and water. It's endless, going past the horizon. The beach doesn't curve or bend. It's just straight, almost like it's a road. It is hot. Too hot. Sweat pours down my neck.

Where am I?

"You really think he can help you?" a woman says on my right. It's Aisling. With her olive skin, wavy black hair, and twinkling green eyes, she's the most beautiful thing I've ever seen. All my senses dial up to eleven as the world around me blurs. The heat drops. My only focus is her warm green eyes. The heat slowly cools.

"Um ... yeah," I respond unwillingly, "I mean, we gotta at least try something, you know?" I have no control of my body or my words. It's like I'm watching myself talk.

"But why?" her face changes. Her voice is now frantic and raspy as she chokes back tears.

What do I do?

"Because we don't got any options," I respond. "It's like Levi said, 'If we have the chance to help a person out, why not take it?'"

"Because Levi's a blazing idiot who has no loyalty, no love for anything! He's much more focused on what alloy he should put in his car's rims than on his own son's well-being."

"What? Where do you get that from?" I'm now in control of my voice. *I don't remember this ever happening? What is this?*

"It doesn't matter," she says flustered, "You were right. I guess ... I guess there's just a certain meanness in this world."

Aisling stands up and walks away from me. The blistering heat returns. Panic swells my chest. "Aye, wait," I yell. "where are you going?" My legs don't move. *Why ain't I chasing her?* My stupid body doesn't move. I'm stuck facing the sea, hanging my head between my legs, defeated. My chest hollows. I close my eyes, turning the world around me to black.

In the dark, a high-pitched ringing blares over the rolling waves. It quickly turns to a sharp pain, like someone's poking needles into my ears. I wake up with a flash. A sea of the color red blocks my vision. Literally, everything around me is tinted. It looks like I'm in a doctor's office or some sort of lab. I'm clamped down to some metal table. Wires and cords sticking out of my body going in every direction. A helmet on my head. "Aisling!" I try to yell, but my voice is scratchy and dry like I ran a marathon without drinking any water. The itching in my throat grows. I cough violently.

I've gotta find her! Where'd they take her? Is she here with me? My restraints are tight. I can't move my arms. I close my eyes and pull. The cold metal of the clamps keeps me down. A slight groan from the metal.

C'mon man! This is your wife we talking about here! Get out! Don't tell me I worked out most of my life for nothing! In a sudden burst, the clamps rip off the table. The momentum carries them into the helmet, smashing it.

Oh shit, I broke metal ... hell yeah! My vision is still red. In it, I can see each possible exit point, a door four meters to the left, each possible weapon, whether it be a knife or a syringe, is highlighted in green. And there's a screen of some kind against the wall.

What is that? On cue, the large monitor is highlighted in blue light. A loading bar appears below it, then the words, "Access Granted."

What the hell? A wave of automated files is thrown at me: a guide on how to use each type of gun, melee weapon, street racing, off-roading, and the types of hand-to-hand combat and stealth training. *Hell no! What?* I try dodging them, but they follow, always staying in eye view. I trip over the table where I was restrained and hit a tray of surgical tools. I crawl backward, away from the monitor. A small clanking sound of metal on metal. Looking down at the noise, there's a cutting tool thing surgeons use sticking out of my hand. Only the tip of the bent blade is inside. I don't feel it. I pull out the blade. There's no pain, no struggle. It's easy. When it exits my hand, no blood. The blade bent and dented like a crushed soda can. My hand is made of metal. Although there is skin, underneath is pure black steel. The small gash on my hand slowly closes, healing itself.

No way this is real? This isn't possible! Skin don't heal like that! The files have stopped flowing through my vision. One is stopped in front of me. The title, "Deal with O'Scandrick." *Deal with O'Scandrick? Like, kill?* It opens automatically and reads, "Levi has agreed to our terms. He has apologized and will since be condemned. If all goes well, our biggest problem will be killed in Nowhere. Sincerely, Leonardo Santos V.8."

"They're going to kill Levi? The same people who took Aisling? Not happening."

"We're not killing anyone, nor did we take Aisling," a scrawny man enters the room. With his beady eyes, neatly trimmed hair, and suit, he looks like a typical corporate douche. He enters the room and goes straight toward the monitor. He presses buttons and levers on his screen and taps his hip. In the sea of red, a small blue light glows from him. As it gets brighter, the tint disappears. The typical colors of the world replace the red.

What the hell just happened?

"Who are you, and where is Aisling?"

"Straight to the point? You know, some would actually admire that?" his voice never wavers from its monotone. He's calm, his hands behind his back. With a beard, I almost didn't recognize him.

"You're Leo. Marshall's pet. Levi—"

"Is alive and well," he interrupts, "although I am not certain how much longer. The Wright Gang tends to be very … Old Testament with their captives."

What the hell is he talking about? I ain't got time for this fool. I sprint at him, prepared to tackle him into the monitor.

A small headache builds rapidly in the back of my skull. It swells, taking over my entire head. I collapse to the floor, rolling around, clenching my head. Leo walks out of view. I close my eyes. All I can do is scream.

The pain slowly dies down. My eyes open. Leo stands at the monitor studying a fancy-looking image of my brain. "Your questions will be answered as we continue our work together, Mr. Jones," his stoic act is really ticking me off.

"You work for Marshall. You took my wife. There's no chance in hell I'm working with you."

"You can choose to do that and risk your brain rejecting its new components, leading to you dying in agony over the course of several hours. Or, you can stay with me, as angry as that makes you, and not only live but help others as well."

"What do you mean brain rejecting new components? What the hell did you do to me?"

Leo's eyes roll to the back of his head like an angry teenager. The tone of his words matches the sass, "I used technology usually reserved for wounded soldiers to ensure you do not die. In their case, they would be sent back out in the field to fight again. You, although doing the same, will be fighting a real war. One caused by two people we both thought we can trust."

"Get to the point, man!"

"I want to help those in Nowhere," he says passionately. "Although this is against my boss's wishes, I feel like you and I, as precarious this relationship may be, will work to do that. To right the wrongs of people we thought were good-natured."

"I never thought that Marshall was a nice guy. He's—"

"I'm not talking about Marshall, in our case, Mr. Jones. Levi's deal. I'm assuming you saw it since you stole hundreds of files from our server—"

"I ain't steal any—"

"He betrayed you and his family in order to spare his own life. My boss wanted him dead for a mistake he made, and in turn, he traded your life for his."

"Oh, don't give me any of that bull, man. Levi would never—"

"You saw the report. He has no loyalty. No compassion. You knew he was an emotionless shell of a man. Is it so far of a reach to believe he had no real connection to …" he pauses for a moment, studying me. "Fine. Don't believe me. Understand that, in Nowhere, there's a certain meanness to this very distinct world. Some of the people out here, dare I say, have lost their humanity." In front of me, a tan holographic map fades into place. It's labeled "Local Map 129: Old Town Colorado."

"You are desperate for answers right now," he continues while zooming in on a house in the woods on the map, "I understand that. And I promise I will give you those answers. But we do not have much time if we are to help. About twenty miles west of here is a holdout for some cannibals," Leo says casually.

"Wait, they're real?"

"Yes, Mr. Jones, they're real," he responds with little patience for my question. He squats down to the floor, meeting me eye to eye, "As of now, most cannibals are out, setting traps inside some of the Other camps nearby, so there will only be a couple inside their little shack. However, one group seems to be breaking that trend, killing now rather than simply trapping them. Just go in, kill the leader Ted, and leave. Once Ted is dead, the other cannibals shouldn't be so hard for the rest of us to track down."

He's not making any sense. Why save me, then immediately throw me into some crazy mission? And his vibe ... Leo's beady eyes stare at me, waiting for a response.

Something's up with this guy. "You do want to help Americans stuck in Nowhere be able to live their best lives, don't you?" Leo asks, interrupting my train of thought. "You strike me as the kind of guy who craves to take advantage of a second life," the words flowing effortlessly out of his mouth, like he's rehearsed this a thousand times.

Just play along. It can't be that bad. View it as a training session for his future ass whooping.

"Of course," I respond. "When do we start?"

CHAPTER 17

WARNING: THE HAPPY PLACE MAY INCLUDE CANNIBALS

JAVIER JONES
DECEMBER 23, 2064

"When they supposed to get here? It's getting late?" I ask, my voice wavering. Aisling sits next to me inside a limousine. She wears a soft blue dress that highlights the lines of her body perfectly. Hundreds of people are around us, some taking pictures, others just cheering.

"Hey, it doesn't matter if they're here or not. We got this, okay?" she says as she checks her reflection in the tinted window.

"You're right," I say shaking. "We'll be fine. Everything's fine. We're fine. One hundred percent fine."

"JJ," she says, her eyes still locked on her reflection, "the more you say it's fine, the less I believe you."

"That's so comforting," I respond quickly.

"Hey," she slides over to me. "I can feel the warmth radiating from her body. The sweet smell of her fruity perfume fills my nose. "All you have to do is stay calm and relax," she says way too calmly, "And if all else fails, I'll just save you like I did last interview."

"I'm telling you, Ace, Levi would've at least helped with my prep. He's good for that," I respond, still shaking.

She glares at me with those soft green eyes, "Sure he would have."

The dream fades, and I'm lying in the bed of an all-black pickup truck. The high trees are dry and brittle but paint a pretty picture with the blue sky. The leaves on the trees are multicolored, mostly brown. The dying grass below is at least a meter high. About fifty meters ahead of me is a small log lodge. Smoke puffs from its chimney and clouds the clear blue sky.

Why do I have to wake up from those dreams? Being with ... uh ... her, it's nice. She's incredible. Something about her is so, I don't know, comforting.

"You fell asleep while driving," Leo's voice blares inside my head.

"Gah, what the hell, man?" I yell back at him. His voice sends shockwaves down my spine. Sitting up in the bed of the truck, I look around but don't see him.

"You fell asleep while driving," he repeats, "Are you sure you're ready to do this?"

"What? Yeah, I want to do it," I respond, "Where you at, anyway?" *Is he in my head?*

"That's not what I asked you. Are you ready to do this? Are you ready to take a life?"

Take a life? Now, why did he have to go say something like that? "Take a life?" I mumble, "You ain't mentioned that before."

"JJ, you're facing cannibals. What did you expect?"

Wait, so he ain't here? Really? He's just gonna let me do this on my own? I can just dip. What's he going to do? Yell at me to death?

"Okay, great," he says without waiting for my response, "Now when you are about to attack, or, with your experience, more likely get attacked, your vision may turn red. Don't panic. It's entirely normal."

"Red?" I ask as I get out of the truck. My head aches as the memory of waking up yesterday plays. "Like what happened when my head was about to explode?" I continue, "That red?"

"Yes. Your head shouldn't hurt this time. All you have to do is go in, kill anyone you see and leave."

"You making it sound so easy," I say insecurely, "What if there's someone in there I shouldn't ... you know." *Am I actually about to do this? It's not like these people are actually cannibals. Those are just myths.*

"Love the arrogance, Mr. Jones," Leo responds, ignoring my question, "but now is not the time. These people are dangerous. Use the targeting system on your interface to lock on to targets."

"Pardon?"

"Shoot the ones that show up yellow. When you lock on to a target, you're shot will curve to hit said target."

"Person," I mumble to myself.

"No, I mean target," Leo responds aggressively.

He continues, "There's a gun in the bed of the truck. We call it the Grim Reaper. A semiautomatic rifle that's linked to your brain. When you want it to shoot, it does it for you. If you want to hit someone from a distance, think "sniper," and it'll transform into a sniper rifle. Combat leads to machine gunfire. There are also three explosives inside as well. Use them carefully, or they will kill you too."

"Couldn't you have come up with a more original name?" I ask, trying to lighten the mood.

"We save lives, Mr. Jones—"

"JJ," I correct.

"We leave the art and creativity to the people who design the Paradise Cities."

Walking to the back of the pickup, I see the rifle strapped to the bed. The black, big barreled gun has purple streaks flowing down the barrel all the way to the butt of the gun. For a weapon, it's pretty gorgeous.

"Where's the ammo?" I ask.

"It's a concept weapon, JJ. It shoots the lasers we use to cut through Leviathan Steel."

"So this can cut through the wall?"

"In theory, yes. Also, in theory, it'll explode if you overwork it."

"So you raise me from the dead just to kill me with my own gun? How's that smart?"

"You were never dead. Now hurry up. Time is of the essence."

Taking the Grim Reaper, I approach the small shack. The grass beneath my feet is knee-high.

In my vision, a recommendation appears, "Duck in high grass."

I obey.

"And hey," Leo's voice shakes me, "don't worry about an unnecessary killing. You are in Nowhere now, JJ. People out here are more animal than person. If they see you, they'll … well … you'll see."

As I get closer, the world around me turns red. A yellow target approaches on the right side of my vision. It's a human, but that's about all I can tell. It looks like one of those persons that tells you to walk on the street signs. *I follow her? Sure*—as she gets closer to the shack. A sight also comes into vision, tracking the distance of the person.

This is actually kinda cool. It's like I'm in a game. Before I pull the trigger, I freeze. *I ain't going through with this. I don't care what Leo says. These are still people. Just cuz the twisted government dismissed them doesn't mean I have to.*

As the person gets closer to the door, she slows. She peers through a window and looks into the shack. *What is she doing?* As I get closer, my computer vision highlights a good-sized stick in her hand. Two more yellow targets come into sight on my right. These ones are much larger than the first. *I can barely see with this stupid thing. How am I supposed to shoot when I can't see what I'm killing? Hey brain, turn this red vision off.*

The red tint vanishes, and the world returns to its normal beautiful colors. A minor headache develops in the middle of my head. The first target, now clearly a middle-aged woman with brown hair, brown eyes, and sun-kissed skin, ducks and runs as the other two approach, only to be intercepted by a third I didn't even see. She struggles to break out of the third person's grip. He's a large man who looks like a Viking. As the small woman struggles, the giant Viking bites down on her arm, forcing her to drop her club.

The other two, a thin teenage girl and a tall, sickly-looking boy, race toward the commotion and drag the small woman inside. The giant wipes the blood off his lips, smiling as it drips from the corner of his mouth.

Did he just ... oh shit. They real. Like actually real. Slowly, I approach the door. The minor headache in my head worsens as the red vision tries to take over, but I beat it down.

"What are you doing?" Leo asks in my head, "Use your targeting system. Do you want to die?"

"My body shivers as a thought of me dying and getting eaten pops into my head. *This guy is the worst conscience ever.* Things are really this bad out here? That people gotta start eating each other like that? Damn, that's some P.R.R.C. level of crazy. *Okay, how am I supposed to deal with legit cannibals? Just attack? Sure.*

I burst through the door. The small woman, now gagged, is sprawled on the table next to a teenage boy with a similar complexion as the small woman. Next to them are maybe ten or more cannibals, all armed to the teeth with guns, knives, and one even has a trident.

For a moment, we all just stare at each other, hesitant to use our weapons. One of the younger cannibal's knees shakes as he stares at me. Another pees himself. Each of their faces stares at me, concerned and, more than that, scared.

Before I can even understand what's going on, the red vision flashes on. I fight it, but no matter how many times I turn it off, it comes back. I can barely catch a glimpse of one of the cannibals moving her hand toward her hip. Is she reaching or …

Before I can even register, the Grim Reaper fires. Within a matter of seconds, every armed person in the room is dead on the floor.

What did I do?

Blood pools up on the wooden floor. Each person's face is blank or, worse, frozen with a horrified look on their face. The teenager's and woman's muffled screams shake me out of my trance. I run over and untie them. The woman grabs the teenager and drags him out of the house.

"C'mon, Mark," she yells at the boy, "More are on their way with that crazy commotion you just caused."

"You can't blame me for that," the boy yells at who I assume is his older sister, "I had to take something to eat! We're starving out here! Dad would never—"

"Ah!" I scream. I'm paralyzed, grabbing my head. I can feel the blood drip out of my ears and down my neck as my headache worsens. My body shivers as the muscles in my back go into a spasm. I collapse onto the floor.

I just killed people. I just ended people's lives. They … they were bad people, but … what if she wasn't reaching—

"JJ!" Leo's voice returns, "JJ can you hear me? I can't help you unless you calm down. You need to calm your mind!"

The faces of the dead I just killed flash in front of me. I just killed … Oh shit … I just killed people. A pair of hands grab my shoulders. They tug on my body, dragging me across the floor to the outdoors. I continue to scream as I'm dragged away. *Happy place. Find a happy place.*

Immediately, I'm switched over to a dream. I'm back in that same limousine from earlier. That woman is sitting next to me, laughing as she pops champagne. Same blue dress as before, but damn, does it still drop my jaw. My head slumped forward. My chest is heavy. A sinking feeling fills my gut.

"Oh, cheer up," she says as she pours herself a glass, "it wasn't that bad."

"Are you kidding me?" I yell back to her. "I was a laughingstock up there! Every person in the auditorium thought I was a mumbling idiot."

"But who cares what they thought," she responds. "They're a bunch of rich snobs anyway." She can barely keep her contorted smile from growing into a stifled laugh as she looks at my pouting face.

She continues, "You know, my first big speech was much worse than this. I was a joke to the men I was speaking to. So, I got drunk and poured my drink on the crotch of one of the shareholders."

I half-heartedly laugh, "Wait, actually? Why would you do that?"

"Because he was a sexist jackass who was more interested in flirting with me than actually listening to my offer."

"So you legit threw your drink on his crotch?"

"The meeting was already going poorly. I knew I was never going to get their investment, and we were already at this over-the-top fancy bar."

"Right, so you had to make a scene," I tease.

She smiles ear to ear. "You're missing the point, fool. Everyone needs to fail once to learn. You failed, and may I say, in spectacular fashion. Now learn."

The dream fades. Standing above me are the woman and the teenage kid from before. The woman hugs the teenager, sheltering him from me. Her eyes are focused and wild.

I failed. Now learn.

CHAPTER 18

OTHER LAND

JANET SIMS
DECEMBER 23, 2064

About a mile or so past the city, Nowhere doesn't begin to live up to its name. This heat wave right now is coming off a couple of weeks of strong, cold rains, making this supposedly hellish landscape look like ... well, a paradise. The road we're on is cracked and riddled with potholes, but inside each crack, grass grows and flowers bloom. Each decaying house has people living inside it wearing awfully mismatched clothes that are either way too big or too small. But the houses look like something out of a fantasy show G.L.E. would produce, with trees growing out of them and moss on the roofs.

Maybe I can make it out here.

The Other hasn't said a word since I shut down his knock-knock joke. He's pale. His sport coat and white shirt are soaking with blood. His eyes are glazed over.

Did I really insult him that badly?

"You okay?" I ask.

"Yeah," he answers too quickly, his voice frail, "I'm just thinking, you know? Why would you want to leave that place? Was it the lights? They were a bit much, don't you think?"

"No, it wasn't the lights. I actually liked those." I can trust him. He hasn't done anything wrong yet. "I was running from the police cuz they thought I, like, killed some crazy restaurant owner."

"Oh," he says sheepishly. He pauses for a moment, his brow contorted, "Did you?"

"No! Of course not! This weird G.L.E. robot dude did, and they wanted to pin it on me."

"Oh," he again says passively. *What is wrong with him?* In the distance, a circular courtyard lights up the darkening sky. Four large apartment buildings surround the circle, sticking out like candles.

What if these Others aren't like him? What if they're—

"Ali's back!" yells a man in the distance. He wears a red and white Hawaiian shirt, has a scraggly beard, black-rimmed glasses, and is bulky. A smile slowly works its way onto the Other's face, who I guess is Ali. As we drive past the first apartment building, I can't count the number of dirty looks I'm getting. Hundreds of people line up on the street or stand on their balconies looking down at me with such hate. Some regrip their guns. Others just look ready for a fight.

The guy in the Hawaiian shirt and glasses approaches Ali as he parks. "I did it, Charlie! Completed my first mission!" he boasts with a sudden burst of energy.

"Congrats, Ali," the guy in the Hawaiian shirt responds dryly. "You just gave a family a chance at a better life." Charlie's eyes have yet to look away from me. He studies me like I'm some piece of art.

"Who's your friend, Ali?" Charlie asks, his eye twitching.

"Janet," Ali pants, "Don't worry, Charlie. She's fine. She actually helped me get out of the city."

Is he lying for me?

"Really?" Charlie says, his disbelief unfiltered, "Cuz she looks like a shiny princess in that sparkly crop top who wouldn't dare get her hands dirty." Ali gets up from the buggy holding his gut.

"If you want to kick her out later, that cool."

No, it's not!

"At least let her rest for a few days. She's been through a …" His eyes roll into the back of his head. Color rushes out of his face.

He's gonna pass out!

Before I can react, Ali collapses on top of me. I close my eyes and put my hands up to protect myself. There's a heavy thud on the side of the car. Slowly opening my eyes, Ali lies passed out on the hood. The Others stare daggers at me. My arms cover my face.

"Some helper, huh?" Charlie mocks. "Joanne! Make sure he's still breathing."

A woman with green hair wearing a bulky leather jacket and jeans runs over. She gives me her best evil eye before putting her finger on Ali's neck. A couple of others follow her and pick him up. They take him into a smaller building in the middle of the circular apartment complex.

All these Others … they hate me. Why would they? Maybe they think I'm, like, I don't know. Well, if they're as out of touch as we're told—

"You planning on getting out of that thing, or do you want to bake in the sun all day?" Charlie asks.

"Um … yeah, definitely, but I just wanted you to know I'm not like the rest of the PC people."

"No?" he responds again, mocking me.

"No," I say sternly as I exit the buggy. "I actually helped people in the city."

"How?" another shouts from a balcony.

For once, please let stereotypes be true.

"Well, I would use Pixie to solve people's problems, which is kinda like what you guys do."

Charlie scoffs at this, "You mean you sneak people past death traps and neo-Nazis in order to give those who can't survive in this harsh climate a chance at a better life."

"Uh … well, no. I used my social network to pinpoint bad things companies do and warn the population about it. That's why they came after me. So …"

Please work. Please work.

The Others look confused. Some mumble to each other. Finally, Charlie breaks the silence.

"Like what?" he asks. "What do you mean? What bad things did you warn the population about?"

"Uh, well, there was this guy using cow meat in his food, killing our planet and …" the Others don't show any sway with the story. If anything, they look angrier.

"What's wrong with cows?" one yells from the back of the crowd.

Oh crap …

"Well, they poison the Earth," I stammer, "because they release methane, so, to protect our planet, I made sure cow meat isn't used."

"That's so typical of those from the Paradise Cities," a skinny ginger approaches. Although short, the man walks with the confidence of a king. Others move out of his way as he approaches me.

Why does this guy look so familiar?

"You said you post on Pixie?" he continues interrogating me.

"Yes."

"Pixie, a social media page designed where each post receives a certain amount of money. The more followers, the more shares, the more money."

This is exactly why I shouldn't listen to stereotypes.

"Well, I had to make money somehow, but that doesn't mean—"

"So you profited off of what you considered someone else's suffering. Which, if I may add, isn't suffering to us. It's survival." The crowd sways with the words of this man. He controls them.

"I didn't mean to—"

"Just like all those that leave the Paradise Cities, she is a fraud. She lies, manipulates, and poses as a hero only to profit off of suffering. She is the Devil!" he screams, his voice cracking, "and the Devil must be punished for her sins!"

Where the hell did that come from? Charlie nods his head. The leader of this coyote group is allowing for this. *What do I do? This one skinny guy's gonna kill me!* "You promised Ali you wouldn't hurt me!" I yell at him.

The red head shoots Charlie a death glare. Charlie refuses to make eye contact with him, instead focusing on me, "Ali is naïve. He is a great kid who we all love, but he is stupid when it comes to who he chooses to help. I did make that promise. However, that was before I learned why you were kicked out of the city. Murder is unacceptable, especially to a man trying to make an honest living."

How does he know that? I didn't tell him that.

The red head's sinister smile reaches ear to ear. In his hand, a Tigress Notebook. On the frame of Charlie's glasses, the head of a tiger. With his neatly trimmed beard and short red hair, I finally recognize him.

This is my way out.

"Charlie, I know you just met me and, well, obviously hate me, but this man isn't an ... uh ... he isn't from Nowhere. He's Leonardo Santos! He's President Marshall's bitch boy! He's evil! He's—"

"I know," Charlie responds. "He's been a great help to us."

I gotta get outta here!

I sprint away, only to run into another Other. This one is different than the rest. He's tall, obscenely pale. His arms long and skinny. Despite the heat, he wears a slim-cut suit. With one move, he wraps his spider-like hands around my neck and slams me to the ground. My heartbeat is in my head. Pressure builds up under my eyes as he squeezes me. Black spots form. I squirm and kick, but my feet only meet empty air.

"Let her go," Leo says. The skinny man releases his grip on my neck. I cough on the floor, gasping.

"Toss her in the Cave," he continues, now glaring at Charlie. "We have more important issues to deal with tonight."

CHAPTER 19

PURPLE SMILES

LEVI O'SCANDRICK
DECEMBER 23, 2064

I wake up lying face up in the grass of the purple forest. There are thousands of stars in the night sky. The purple lighting projects its color onto everything around it, turning the large redwood a deep shade of purple.

Where am I?

Although my legs touch the high grass on the forest floor, I cannot feel it. "Hello," I yell. My voice falters. I try speaking again, but it's a dry heave. In the distance, the low sound of string instruments sweeps through the air, followed by the familiar sound of a child's laughter.

Jackson? The echo of the music continues to play, followed again by my son's laughter. *Jackson!*

I sprint in the direction of the noise. The music disappears. All I can hear are voices echoing through the forest all around me. They come from every direction. Jackson laughs in front of me. Aisling spits a dry joke to my left. Then my right. JJ mocks something about my disgruntled appearance. Kaiya …

Hearing my wife's voice is like breathing in the fresh ocean air. It jolts me out of my trance and fills me with anticipation. With a tugging sensation in my chest, like someone's pulling me forward, I launch into the night sky and come face to face with the G.L.E. logo. The smiling moon is the light source for this world, illuminating the sky and Earth with its purple hue. The smile is not one of joy but mockery. Its slanted eyes and gaping mouth relax into its permanent smile. Its cartoonish grin grows along with my confusion.

What is this? Was I captured by G.L.E.? Are they torturing me?

Within a moment, the moon throws me back down to Earth.

I land on my feet at the edge of the forest. In a small gap in the trees, Kaiya and Jackson play as JJ and Aisling bring food out to the picnic table. In this little slab of open space in the dense forest, they seem to be enjoying themselves, smiling like there's not a care in the world.

They can't be here. This can't be real. I look down at my body. I move my left leg, then right. I twist my wrist. I think I am in control of myself. *Maybe this is the afterlife.*

Smiling, I take a step toward my family. But before I can reach the table, I'm stopped by an invisible wall. Around my waist, a large black collar. Its chain goes back a mile into the forest. Then out of the ground, a deep rumbling sound. The earth shakes. My family doesn't seem to notice.

The wall erupts out of the ground, throwing me backward. I land on my ass. The now fully erect Leviathan metal behemoth glistens in the purple light, separating me from my family. Despite being on the other side, their voices are still clear. They laugh and giggle, not even noticing my disappearance. It's like they don't even care I'm not there.

The more their joy grows, the more painful it becomes. It feels like a hot steel rod is being shoved down my body. I crumble to the floor, tearing at my ears, accepting this is my life for the rest of eternity. I played my cards, and this is what I get for it.

The ground beneath me morphs into a chair. It raises me from the ground and clamps on to my head and arms, forcing me to look straight at the wall. A tiny window allows me to peep inside, showing me the life I threw away.

"The worst way to die is when you're lying on your death bed and, looking back at your life, realizing, you lived a life full of regret, and knowing there's nothing you can do to change it." My dad's words echo in my head on repeat. The eternal humiliation I've earned myself. This is simply who I am and always was. The outsider, the man playing father and friend when really, I should never have even been allowed to try in the first place.

A hot splash of water smacks my face, and my eyes flutter open. The sound of deep growling and howls take over my family's laughter. As my vision clears, I'm in a cage, back in the real world surrounded by a bunch of jackasses with red falcons on their white clothes.

Never mind. This is hell.

"Levi O'Scandrick," a tall, muscular man says slowly as he approaches me. His all-white clothes are way too shiny and clean. The large red falcon tattooed to his hairy chest matches the one on his low-cut robe. All I can do in response is groan.

"Ha!" the large man laughs. "I thought you would be more formidable of a threat, but instead, you are smaller than the sandwich I had for lunch." There are maybe twenty or so Wright Gang members surrounding me. Each looks the same, bald head, big muscles, fragile ego.

"Jackson," I'm able to spit out, "Kaiya ... where is my family?"

"Oh, they are fine," Muscle Man answers. "Kaiya's in a better place. Rest in peace."

"Rest in peace," the rest of the Wrights answer. "And Jackson is alive and well," Muscular Man answers.

"He's alive?" I say, a sudden burst of energy shoots through my body. I jump at the cage wall only to be met with a powerful electric shock. The Wrights laugh as I slam back to the floor.

He's alive. If that's true, I have to get out of here. Where is he? Where would Marshall take him?

"Where is he?" The taste of metal in my mouth is potent.

"Hmm," Muscle Man taunts. "I think I remember him being shipped off to California, working in an old Russian agricultural field."

No. This can't be happening. They're going to kill him there. Getting into California ... it's impossible.

"Now, Levi," Muscle Man says with confidence, "President Marshall wants me to search you for some flash drive that has important information on it and then kill you. But I honestly couldn't give a crap about that. What I want is for the engineer that designed the wall and created the robotic police to do the same for us. Give us a weapon we can use to destroy this wasteland and cleanse it in the name of God!"

The Wrights cheer loudly. Some howl, others stomp their feet and clap. One idiot shoots his gun in the air.

I have nothing. I have nothing. My family is dead. Jackson is going to be tortured for the rest of his life ... The flash drive's heavy in my pocket. *All of them are dead for this? What is on it that's so important? Doesn't matter. I'm done.*

"Can you skip the big boasting speech and get to the part where you just kill me," I say, slurring my speech.

Muscle Man laughs. "Sure," he says slowly. He throws more water onto my cage, getting me and the ground wet. Some of the water gets into my mouth. It's salt water.

Another one of the large men drags a sparking wire toward the cage. He places it down on the water, electrocuting me. I scream as the energy fries my body. The pain is immeasurable. The heat from the electricity makes my blood boil. The electric current sends pins and needles through my entire body. My gut feels like it's being cooked on five-hundred-degree heat. The point of contact with the frayed wire seemingly melts.

The man pulls the wire away from the water, stopping the current. I fall back down onto the floor. A metallic taste in my mouth. The scent of smoking flesh.

"Or," Muscle Man says, "you can do us a favor. Build us our weapon. Something we can use to cleanse the wasteland and eventually the Paradise Cities of the filth that claims inside of it."

"How 'bout a car?" says another.

"Sure, a car sounds delightful," Muscle Man responds.

Kaiya and Jackson playing in that purple sky flashes in my brain. Their smiles and laughter warm my charred heart. "Or you could just kill me," I'm barely able to say.

Muscle Man looks confused like he's never seen a person who wants to die. He gestures to the man with the wire, who throws it back onto the water. The electric current is excruciating. The smell of my cooking flesh overwhelms my senses. One good thing. If I'm going to die, just do one good thing so I don't live a life of complete regret. Give them the weapon they desire. Then, kill them, ridding the world of a good chunk of assholes.

"Fine!" I yell. The man pulls away the wire. I lie gasping on the ground, spraying water with each breath I take.

"I'd knew you'd come around," Muscle Man says, smirking. "We'll give you one week, Levi."

"Three days," I wheeze out, "then promise you'll kill me quickly."

Muscle Man contemplates the issue. His block head and beefy neck don't match his "high" level of "thought."

"Very well," he responds. "You keep your end of the deal. We'll keep ours. All the tools you'll need will be in the garage. You will eat, sleep, and shit making this car, understand? We have a specimen already there for you to work on. It's American, of course."

"Of course," I whimper out.

Some of the other Wright Gang members put on gloves, grab my cage, and push me away. Muscle Man smiles and says his final words to me, "It was a pleasure to do business with you, Levi. A genuine pleasure."

You have no idea how much of a pleasure it will be for me.

CHAPTER 20

THE BAD GUY

ALI SCHOLTZ
DECEMBER 26, 2064

"You're going to get Levi O'Scandrick, and you're going to bring him here," Charlie says to me as I lie on the hospital bed.

I stare at him and the weird-looking man behind him. The weird guy has his head pointed up to the ceiling and his hands behind his back. He stands perfectly straight. His fiery red hair neatly combed. He looks like a cartoon meerkat. "You're joking?"

"No, Ali, we could benefit from having a guy like that here. He can help us figure out the best way to equalize Nowhere and the PC's."

The weird man is really distracting. He keeps looking at his hip, then back at me, and then to Charlie. "Who's that?" I ask. Charlie slaps his hand to his forehead, "That's Dennis. He's a friend of ours from the Salt Dune's down in Utah."

"And he's coming with me?" I ask, confused.

"No, he's not," Charlie says, frustrated.

"And why me? I'm not completely healed. Dr. Jesus said I need like three more—"

"I don't care what Joanne said!" Charlie screams.

See, Ali. This is why you don't ask too many questions. Now he's mad.

"I'm sorry, Charlie," I say quietly. "I'll go right away."

"Thank you," he says, still angry. He takes a backpack and puts it on the bed.

The weird-looking guy, Dennis, walks over to me. "We need him back alive, Ali, you understand?" He talks like Charlie does when he's had a bad day. Rough, gets mad about anything, and just mean.

"I know. That's how I do things," I respond.

"Now, when you get there," Dennis says to me like I'm a baby, "you will just have to sneak in through the air ducts. We really don't know the landscape of the place."

"So, what's the rhyme?" I ask.

Dennis stares at me, confused, "Excuse me?"

"The rhyme? The jingle? There's a rhyme and a timer so I can know the direction I need to go in and out of safe and sound."

"What?" Dennis looks at Charlie. "What's he talking about?"

Charlie pulls Dennis to the side. They mumble to each other for a moment. I've never seen Charlie so stressed. He's sweating, and his hand has yet to stop rubbing his face. He can't stand still either. He keeps switching feet, going back and forth like it's a hot summer, one-hundred-and-forty-degree day.

Why is Charlie letting this guy bully him? That's so unlike him.

"Fine!" Charlie yells to Dennis, who finally grins.

Charlie, with a strained look on his face, says through his teeth, "It's the Wright Gang, Ali. We're sending you into the Wright Gang headquarters in Ohio."

"Wait, wait, wait," I stammer, "Hold on a second. The Wright Gang? Are you kidding me? Alone? Charlie, you know I got all the respect in the world for you, but are you crazy! I'm going to die in there! And no plan? I mean—"

"Ali," Charlie's voice is calm and firm, "we don't have another option. You're the best we've got right now. All of us are counting on you."

"Ah, why'd you have to go and say something like that?"

Charlie smiles. For a faint moment, the wrinkles around his eyes disappear, and he looks like his old self again.

"All right," he says, "now go get dressed. We've got all the weapons and armor you need in there." He wraps me in a bear hug and says, "Come back, buddy. Okay?"

"Of course, Charlie," I say, a bit taken back by the affection, "I always do."

He pulls away. The wrinkles are back around his sad eyes. "And, if you don't mind," I say loud enough for Dennis to hear, "I don't really like that Dennis guy. He seems so off."

Charlie chuckles and then says, "Yeah. He's from Utah." He starts laughing as if that's something funny. I laugh too.

I really gotta start learning more jokes.

Charlie and Dennis leave me alone in the room. I get up and start to change into, ah, the same clothes as before. They're at least clean now. The gray jeans have even more holes, and my shirt is in tatters. On top of them is body armor. Some for my legs and my chest. No helmet or arms, though.

This is probably the best they could do. Next to the armor is a large rifle, two pistols, and a couple of real grenades. Ten boxes of ammo lie next to them. *Well, now what am I supposed to do? I can't sneak if there's the loud banging of a gun.* I unzip the backpack. On top of all the tranquilizer rounds in the world is a note written in Charlie's handwriting. "I know how you roll."

I smile at that. That Dennis guy doesn't get what we do here. I don't know about Utah, but here in Pennsylvania, we actually have a heart.

All right. Plan. Wright Gang is bad. I'm just gonna assume they have guards, um, everywhere. So maybe sneak in through the front by distracting in the back. I grab two explosive grenades and stuff them in the pack. I also fill the right tube on the backpack with hurt grenades. Definitely gonna need black smoke. I don't think they'll know it's not poisonous. So big grenade, big grenade, black spoke, hit them close. Hurt grenade on the nearest wall. Ooh, and then hit another side with two hurt grenades timed fifteen seconds apart. Enter front-side. Get into the air ducts and find Levi. Escape through air ducts. If I see anyone, trank them.

I grab the two pistols and load them with the dart clips. I stuff the entire pack with ammo. And put in a couple of black smoke grenades for good measure.

As I finish armoring up, there's a knock on the door. "One sec," I say as I button the vest that's a bit too large for me. I walk over to the door and open it. It's Dr. Jesus. "Oh, hey, Dr. Jesus," I say cheerfully. Her green eyes twinkle as I smile at her.

Keep cool. Don't do that weird thing where I stare too long at her.

"For the last time, Ali, my name is Joanne. Not Jesus," Jesus says in her nasally voice. Her smile is contagious.

"I know. Jesus sounds better," as I stare into her eyes. *Hey! Stop staring.* I clear my throat and stuff the Glocks in my pants. *Say something cool,* "You here to see me off?"

Dr. Jesus looks down the hallway before closing the door. She pulls out a vial from her purse and hands it to me. "Before you go against the Wright Gang, take this. It'll help numb you so your ... well, everything doesn't hurt you when you're fighting them."

"Oh, thanks, Dr. Jesus," I say happily. "What is it?"

"Numbing agent," she says. "It blocks the nerve just enough for you to still move about but also not feel normal amounts of pain."

"Wow." *Try to sound smart.* "That's, uh, that sounds dangerous."

"It's not," Dr. Jesus says, kind of angrily.

Oh man, did I insult her?

Her eyes soften, and she kisses my cheek. Her lips send a warm tingle down my body. "Please," she says smiling, "come back in one piece."

Holy shit, holy shit, holy shit, holy shit, holy shit, holy shit.

She smiles and walks out the door. As she's about to leave, she turns around and says, "You know, I'm glad you changed your mind on that PC trash. If I didn't know better, I would say you're becoming quite the man, Ali. You're no longer some immature kid."

"You like that?"

She blushes and says, "I do."

Holy shit, holy shit, holy shit, holy shit. Wait? Change my mind on what?

"Hey, Dr. Jes—"

Be mature.

"Um, Joanne, what did I change my mind on again?"

"Sending the trash to the Cave," she says. Her smile changes to a serious look, "You did that right?"

"Um, oh yeah," I say, trying to hide my lie. "It's just the drugs made me forget things, you know?"

"Sure," she says, a confused smirk across her face. She turns around and walks away.

She didn't buy that for one second. But why would Charlie lie to me? This isn't like him. New plan. See if Dr. Jesus lied. Then free Janet, or don't free Janet, and she dies. Either way, I'm committing a big no-no. *Just go get Levi. He's the mission. Janet's fine. Charlie wouldn't lie to me.*

I walk out of my room toward the exit. All my comrades cheer me on and pat me on the back as if I just did something great.

Some yell, "Way to go, Ali!"

Another says, "Go kick Wright ass."

I smile at them and dap them up. *They've never been this excited before.* I walk out to the parking lot. The buggy from three days ago hasn't moved. I walk over to it and place the backpack down.

Review plan: Hit the back, so I go front. Easy. Easy, easy, easy.
What if Janet's hurt?
No, brain. Stop. Charlie wouldn't hurt her.
It's on the way. Just check.
No! Review plan, then go kick some Wright ass.
But you're gonna drive right past it anyway. Just check.
Fine!

I start the buggy and head out of the apartment complex. Instead of going left to Levi, I turn to Janet. The Cave looks even more intimidating than normal. Its cave walls reflect the hot morning sun. Three guards stand at the mouth. Its wet interior drips water onto a prisoner with an electrified collar on her. It's Janet.

Oh no. No, no, no. This has to be a mistake. Charlie wouldn't lie. Charlie doesn't lie. That's what he does. But there she is, shivering in the icy cave.

Another buggy approaches. It's Charlie and Dennis. I put my buggy in reverse, park it behind a building.

Charlie and Dennis exit and approach Janet. They don't enter the Cave but turn off the climate. The water stops dripping. Janet still lies on the ground, shivering.

Is this a test? No, it can't be. I'm gone. I'm supposed to be gone.

Dennis walks into the cave and pulls out some sort of heat glove thing. He puts it on his hand. As he enters the Cave, steam burns off his glove.

Oh man, what am I doing?

I jump into the buggy and floor it. The battery pulses as it launches forward. Pulling out one of the pistols, I shoot the three guards in the neck with a trank. They fall to the ground. Dennis spins around and whips out his own pistol, but I shoot him before he has the chance to do the same. As he falls, his glove lands on Janet's leg, burning her. She roars in pain before sliding away.

"Ali!" Charlie yells, "Stop!"

I slam on the brakes and skid forward. Charlie doesn't move as the buggy approaches him. It stops within an inch of him. Jumping out of the buggy, I point the Glock at Charlie. He doesn't flinch. "Let her go, Charlie," I say, mimicking his serious voice.

"You can't be serious, Ali," his face totally calm. "She's the bad guy! Don't you get that? They watch us starve and kill ourselves, and you want to save her?"

"Just let her go," I say, pointing my Glock in his face, "I don't know what that Dennis guy has over you, but this isn't you."

Get closer, unlock her, and run for it.

I step slowly toward the Cave. Charlie mirrors my movement.

"She's part of the problem, Ali," Charlie continues to say. "That's what I've been trying to tell you. You don't kill members of your own team. But she broke that rule simply by living there and leaving us for dead." I get closer to the Cave. Charlie to the buggy.

Please don't make me shoot you. Tears wad up in my eyes. *Control yourself, Ali. Stay focused.*

"What have I always told you," Charlie says, now standing next to the buggy, "'You can't blame a person for where they were born, but only for what they do.' And what did she do, Ali? Not a damn thing."

I am now next to Janet. I unlock the collar on her neck. She collapses backward, barely conscious. Ice burns scar her neck. Picking her up, I head toward the buggy. Charlie doesn't move. He just stares at me as I walk up to him.

"Move," I say.

"She's using you, Ali," he says seriously. "And she'll use you until there's nothing left. Once she's had her fill, she'll dump you like she does to everyone she knows."

"That's my choice," I say. The sound of multiple buggy's driving to us distracts me. Around the apartments, twelve speed toward us.

Seeing an opportunity, Charlie jumps at me, knocking me down. I drop Janet and the gun. He punches me in the mouth repeatedly. He's really strong, each hit ringing my head, blurring my vision. I block another blow and swing back, only for him to grab my arm and pin me.

Charlie tugs my arm, yanking it out of its socket. *He's going to break it.* As the pain reaches its climax, Charlie releases his grip. A trank dart is firmly stuck in his neck. Janet stands wobbly, pointing the Glock. She looks at the gun, shocked. He falls to the ground.

"Thank you," I say. She doesn't speak and grabs one of the big grenades from the buggy. Before I can stop her, she tosses it at my friends. It explodes, missing the vehicles, but causing a massive ash cloud to cover the sky. Metal crashing into metal.

"Ali," Janet's now raspy voice encourages. She sits in the back, holding a pistol.

I jump into the buggy, start it, and drive off. Looking back at my home, a lump forms in my throat as I try to choke back tears. *What did I do?*

"Are you okay?" Janet's raspy voice shakes me out of my trance.

Her big eyes are empty like her life's been sucked out of her.

She needs a win.

"Yeah," I say, forcing a smile onto my face. "Let's go get Levi. I think he may be able to turn things around."

CHAPTER 21

LIBERATION DAY

LEVI O'SCANDRICK
DECEMBER 26, 2064

Two more minutes until liberation.

I've always imagined myself being able to reap the rewards of my greatest accomplishment. But this will have to do. Jackson's laugh continues to play on repeat in my head. He and Kaiya are sitting in the purple world waiting for me. And I'm going to get there. Today, I'm going to get there.

"So what we gonna call it?" asks Bon. The excruciatingly dumb mechanic for the Wright Gang has been on watch dog duty. He's supposed to be learning everything I know in the three days I've agreed to be alive. Like that's possible.

"How about the Good Life?" I ask. I genuinely couldn't care less, but calling my impending death the Good Life just feels so right.

"Nah. That sounds like some PC shit," he says with his thick Louisiana drawl. "How about Bonnie?"

"So … your name?"

"No, my name is Bon, not Bonnie."

"Right," I say, oh so enthused by this ecstatic conversation. Can I at least die next to someone with any resemblance of a brain?

"Now," he asks, "how often do we have to charge it?"

"You don't," I respond quickly, trying to keep his attention away from the overcharged lithium bomb I call my engine.

"Well, if your—" he starts to look at the closest battery.

"No!" I yell a bit too loudly, but it's too late. He sees the timer ticking. 1:28 left. So damn close.

"Yur tryna blow us to hell, Levi?"

"Well, I figured I'm going to die anyway, so I might as well take you with me. You know, to meet your white power God."

He reaches under the metallic purple coup and stops the timer.

Guess I have to do it manually.

The tall cylindrical garage is cluttered with old Cadillac machinery, extra spherical wheels, and Leviathan steel. Bottles of water and booze cover the areas of the floor that aren't blanketed with scrap metal and tools.

Where'd I put that remote?

As I scan the room, the massive garage doors slide open, accompanied by the sound of gunfire. Deinós enters the room along with ten gang members.

"Levi O'Scandrick," he says in his deep, slow speech.

Does he always have to say my name like it's some sort of proclamation?

"Muscle Man, how are we?" The thick steel garage door slams closed, sending a loud echo through the garage. Deinós doesn't react to my comment. His pale eyes stare into mine like he's trying to drink my soul like another protein shake.

"We've encountered a little friend of yours," he says, definitely happy by the news.

"Friend?" I ask, "I don't have any. You know that."

"Well, it seems you have one remaining." Deinós points to the top of the garage. A holographic screen appears, showing a young man fighting the entire Wright Gang. With his dark complexion and bright blond hair, he looks so familiar.

Oh, shit, the kid from the monorail. "I honestly have no idea who that is."

Deinós smiles, obviously pleased with my answer, "So you wouldn't mind if we kill him?"

"Kill away," I say.

Where's the fucking remote? I whip my head around to the workbench. On the corner, under a belt, is the blinking green detonator. *Gotcha.*

"Hey, Tim," Muscle Man announces into a PA system. "Kill him."

The kid freezes and looks around him. "How, sir?" I assume Tim responds over the PA system.

Muscle Man looks me dead in the eye and says, "Drown him in hot tar." On the screen, the kid's entire body deflates as if he's sick of being threatened to be drowned in hot tar.

Get the detonator.

As the Wright Gang members all watch the kid fight off a hoard of gang members, I slowly pace back to the large workshop table.

"So tell me, Levi," Deinós queries, "your time is up. What have you made me?" His eyes are locked on to the screen, watching this one kid dominate the Wright Gang.

Who the hell?

"The Good Life, is the name Bon and I came up with. It's the perfect blueprint for mass production, allowing for your conquest to be quick and efficient." With each word, I inch closer. Bon eyes me curiously.

"It is a purple two-door coupe," I continue, "as requested by Bon. It has spherical wheels that allow it to move in any direction. The wheels are made of dense rubber, so no amount of bullets can cause it too much harm. Four batteries fuel the car. Each is placed next to a wheel and feeds its power directly to said wheel. The coupe is a four-seater like a typical American sports car, with the seats in the back made for the smallest of people. The car is manually driven, so there is an actual steering wheel. Although autodrive is still an option."

Bon's curiosity is peaking. He slowly approaches me.

"The AI system inside the car as of now is registered to me, only so I know the car's diagnostics at all points. With this AI system, the car can shoot with its four machine guns, drop landmines out of the trunk, and spill oil, then promptly light it on fire. Speaking of land mines, the sports car has a V-shaped bottom, so if the car does get hit, little damage will be done. Lastly, it's made of Leviathan steel, which I can only assume Marshall gave you, so it's basically indestructible."

"How many horses?" Deinós asks. He switches off the screen and looks at me. I'm within an inch of the table. Bon stands next to me. His eyes studying mine.

Right, he's a meat head. Should've led with horsepower.

"All four batteries produce about twelve hundred," Bon answers for me, "But, sir, the engines are nuclear. He made it a bomb."

"A bomb?" Deinós says, impressed. "That's awesome! So we can send this bad boy into PC Indi, for example, and it'll blow the whole place up?"

"Sir, I think you—"

"Exactly," I interrupt Bon. "Like you said, you wanted something to destroy the cities with."

When I'm within a couple of inches, Bon catches on to my actions. His eyes widen as he locks on to the detonator. *If I grab the detonator, he can rip it out of my hands before I have a chance to blow it. Gotta delay him.*

"Aye!" he yells as he runs at me. I dive for a broken pipe on the workbench. I turn around only for Bon to run right into the sharp end. The pipe impales him in the stomach. His blood shoots through the other side onto my chest.

Bon stumbles backward, gasping. His big eyes lose their fury as he stares at the pipe protruding from his chest. He struggles to grab me, pulling the pipe further into his body, bringing me closer to him. One of the other gang members drags Bon's dying body to the other side of the garage. Deinós walks up to me, his face beat red. The detonator's green light flashes in my peripheral vision.

Not yet.

As Deinós grabs my neck, there's a loud bang on the thick steel garage doors. Deinós focuses on the rattling doors. He turns on the screen, still wrangling me. An automated forklift rams into the door on repeat. There is no driver. The kid is nowhere in sight.

Now. I try sticking out my hand to grab the detonator. My short arms can't reach. *C'mon! Grab the damn thing! Do you want to see your family again?*

My arm strains. Muscles tear as I overextend. Throwing my body behind it, I swing at the table. As I do, I knock the detonator to the ground. It lands on the garage floor with a hollow clank.

Deinós turns his head only to be met with my fist. *I will see my family.*

He drops me as he grabs his bleeding nose. I land next to the detonator. As I'm about to grab it, a flash flies over the screen. Sparks fly, and wires fall as the ceiling collapses. Then, following the roof, comes the kid from the monorail. He falls from the ceiling, landing on the back of one of the Wrights. The gang member drops to the floor, a needle protruding from his neck.

A smirk crawls onto his face. "Hi!" he says joyously, waiving at the leaders of the Wright Gang.

What the fuck?

Deinós's hands clamp down on my shirt. He tosses me across the room, far away from the detonator. I slam into a workbench. Tools crash on top of me as I spill onto the floor. My head rings, vision blurry. Deinós yells something at the monorail kid, but I can't make it out.

A gang member yanks me off the ground. The cold steel of a gun pressed against my head. The detonator was about thirty feet in front of me. *If I can start a fire while they fight, the heat should ignite the lithium. It won't be the explosion I hoped for, but it can still work.*

Bullets fly as the kid jumps behind a work bench and yells, "Wait! I'm only here for Levi! The rest of you are ... well not fine, cuz ... but safe!"

"You really think we're that stupid?" Deinós yells back as he fires more bullets at the kid. He stops, "If you're really just here for Levi, then you wouldn't mind if we kill him!"

Am I even as smart as I think I am? I don't think so. If I was, it shouldn't have been this much of a struggle to end these idiots.

"That makes no sense," the kid yells.

"Fine!" Deinós yells back, "Then we'll kill you instead!"

Oil and fire. I can't focus. My adrenaline is too high, blurring my vision, my heart pulsing through my entire body. *I need more time.* "See, this is what happens when you try too hard to be an animal," I antagonize Deinós. "Your words don't work no good."

"Shut up, you," the Wright Gang member holding me whispers into my ear. He slams me face-first onto the concrete floor. He presses his palm onto my skull, my head ready to pop like a grape. "When I'm done killing your friend here," he continues, "Imma skin you with a butter knife. Then, Imma—"

The Gang member freezes mid-sentence. The pressure on my head releases. Looking up, the Gang member's eyes roll to the back of his head as he falls on top of me. A pink dart sticks out of his neck.

Shit!

I try pushing him off, but he's too heavy.

A foot stomps next to my face. A young woman dressed in sparkly attire stands above me. With her curly reddish-brown hair, milky white skin, and green eyes, she doesn't look like anyone I've seen in Nowhere. She shoots at another gang member but misses. Before he can recover, the kid from the monorail hits him with a pink dart. He then runs at the girl and jumps behind a workbench. Bullets fly. Deinós' gibberish taunts are silenced by the gunfire. The kid shoots back, the girl hides behind the bench.

C'mon. Get him off me!

My arms strain, my core tightens. I hold my breath and push. The Gang member lifts off the ground about an inch high, but I'm able to slide out.

Where's the detonator?

Thick black smoke fills the air. The bullets have stopped flying. The screams have ceased. With his hand gripping the detonator a couple of meters away from me, Deinós lies motionless. Two pink darts stick out from his neck.

"Where'd he go?" a nasally female voice asks.

Crap! They actually beat Deinós? Who the hell are these kids? I crawl over to the detonator and pry it from Deniós' fingers. *Family, here I come.*

"Hey, Levi, you all right?" the kid from the monorail says.

I flip over on my back. My face may be worse than I thought because the kid jumps, startled. I make an effort to show the kid the detonator in my hand. His eyes lock on to it.

"Now," I say with labored breathing, "you are going to tell me who you are, what you want, and why I'm seeing you again."

"Oh, okay," he says like a child, "I'm Ali. That's Janet."

"Hi," Janet says with the enthusiasm of a rock. Her nasally voice is strained. A burn mark circles her neck.

"We are not here to hurt you." Ali continues, "Just free you from the Wright Gang and … well, ask you to help us."

This has trap written all over it.

"Look," Janet says, "we're not your friends. We honestly don't like you, but we need you to do one thing that'll help hundreds of people out. Can you do that?"

Janet's hand lies heavy on her pistol.

I have a chance to help people. That's what she's asking. She looks like a typical PC princess, but he, he seems like a naïve kid.

Jackson and Kaiya's laughter ring in my head again. The stinging guilt boiling inside my chest is unbearable, "No," I yell. "I can't. I have to see my family again. I'm the bad guy, remember? One good deed, then the wall will go down."

As I'm about to push the detonator, the young kid shoots me in the neck with a dart. Immediately, my eyelids become heavy. My body gains a million pounds as I drop to the floor like a rock.

Ali says, "Bad guys deserve a happy ending too."

No! I have to do this!

My arms don't respond to my wishes. The detonator lying in my palm. Stars cover my vision, making the last thing I see Janet picking up the detonator and looking at the Good Life.

I'm sorry.

CHAPTER 22

BIG DOGS

MARK MORALES
DECEMBER 26, 2064

I can't believe I'm sitting next to Javier Jones. If this situation was better, I would be in total awe. I mean, this guy's the *man*. Like, what kind of dude plays an *entire football game* on a broken leg? One badass mother fucker.

But sitting next to him, he looks kinda wimpy. I mean, I hate to say it, but it's true. He sits slouched over next to my mom under the trees. His hands are on his head. His eyes are wide, like he's having the longest staring contest ever. His warm hazel eyes glisten in the Indianapolis sun.

Stop.

They've been talking for hours. Lord knows about what. I don't get it either. Why is he so sad? And why is he out here? I mean, yeah, the entire world thinks he and his whole squad got killed by those Chinese terrorists at that talk show, but why here?

Should I go talk to him?

Taking a deep breath, I walk over.

My mom's voice slowly fades in, "but that doesn't mean it's your fault."

"I get that, Arianna, but—" he stops when he sees me. "Glad you can join the conversation," he continues with a slight grin. "Mark, right?"

"Uh, yeah," I mutter weakly.

"Your mom says you're a big fan. Says when you're not shooting people in your military video games, you're watching football," he says. I shoot her a look. Why does she always have to embarrass me?

"How are you handling all this?" he continues.

Don't sound weak. "It's nothing," I boast, "wasn't even that bad." His eyes sink as I say that.

Mom shoots me her, "you idiot," look. *Like she can talk.*

"Where are you going?" I ask abruptly.

"Mark," Mom interrupts, "that's none of our—"

"Here actually," he interrupts, "I was sorta sent here to kill the cannibals that were about to eat you."

Wait ... I stole from cannibals?

Mom and I exchange hate-filled glances before I say what I want anyway, "Well, thank God you made it."

"Yeah," he mutters.

Silence follows. I don't get him. He was just the ultimate badass and killed a bunch of heavily armed people. I mean he's supposed to be the toughest man alive, not some bitch.

"What?" JJ says, confused.

Oh crap, did I say that out loud?

"Yeah, it's done," he says to no one.

"Uh, JJ, who are you talking to?"

"Leo," he says as if that answers all the questions. He continues, "Two people who I saved. Well, they actually saved me. You're too kind, Leo. Where? Great, I'll see you there." He stops talking to "Leo" and looks at my mom.

I think he's had too many concussions.

"Do you guys wanna come with me to help more people?" he asks.

"What are you talking about?" Mom asks, seemingly repulsed by the idea. "Well, I was dead as you," he looks at me, "until Leo turned me into a soldier trying to fix this." He gestures to the world around us.

"Now, I go around Nowhere helping people. You guys wanna join me, save a couple of lives? If not, that's fine."

"Yes!" I say too enthusiastically. I clear my throat and lower my voice, "I mean, yeah. Definitely, man."

"Cool. The car's this way," he gets up and walks deeper into the forest. He's definitely distracted. Something's got him pretty messed up.

My back aches with each step I take. The smack I took from that bat the Other used was something else. Then getting hog-tied ... I can't.

My breathing is sporadic. I can feel the pulse in my fingertips. A hand yanks my arm. I jump back only to see its Mom.

"This is not okay," she says, flustered, "He's obviously not okay in the head, and if we're going to make it out here, we need to talk through things and work together, okay?"

Typical. I can't show I'm scared. I'm not scared. I'm fine. Be tough like Dad and don't show any fear.

"Look, mom, we're fine," I say sternly. "He's JJ! Plus, it won't hurt to have a badass soldier around."

JJ hollers from his massive black pickup, "You coming or what?" Before Mom could say anything, I run. The matte black raised pickup truck is massive. I have to jump get in. Mom follows suit.

"All right," I say, grinning uncontrollably, "where to now?"

"Somewhere in Pennsylvania," he says. "Apparently, there's going to be some trouble there."

Smiling, JJ slams on the gas, and the truck launches forward, off to Pennsylvania. No more playing victim. I know I can be more than that. I'm not some bum that can be kicked to the curb. I'm working with the man nicknamed "Superman." I can do this. I can be somebody important.

***

Six hours later, we arrive at the destination. Unlike Indiana, Pennsylvania is a dry desert. Heat waves bounce off the barren ground. Every building in sight looks like a stale cracker.

Further down the road, there are six apartment buildings clustered together in the distance. Their once white walls look gray. The road we drive on is cracked and broken. Dead weeds cover the concrete.

Well, this is a real shithole.

A redheaded man stands in the shade of a house. He's really scrawny and weak but stands with a fat amount of confidence. I can definitely whoop his ass if need be. *But he could be a cannibal. JJ said he was hunting them.* He's definitely staring us down, looking for a fight. *Sweet, my first brawl. I can't wait.* JJ rolls the truck to a stop next to the redheaded man. He gets up from the wall and walks over to the car.

Here we go.

"You all right?" the skinny redhead asks JJ. "Yeah, just a little shook, that's all," he responds to the neatly groomed ginger.

Wait, what?

"You look like you've seen the devil, which I'm guessing means you finally understand what this place really is." JJ nods, his eyes hung low. "Who are these two?" the ginger asks JJ. He gestures for us to exit the truck. We comply. For some odd reason, JJ seems to listen to this skinny twig. It doesn't make sense. They also stand the same too, their heads high, hands behind their back, feet close together.

"This is Arianna," JJ says, "and this is her son Mark Morales. They were about to be eaten by the cannibals before I got there."

"Eaten?" the ginger asks, acting taken aback, "This is usually trapping season, not eating season. I'll have to keep a look at that."

"Trapping season?" I ask. The weird man tries staring me down, and I stare right back. Nobody's intimidating me out here.

"Yeah, trapping season," he says, "when they catch people and store them in their basements or farms. Herd them like sheep until they're ready to eat them."

Like sheep? Human farms? What the hell is this place? The weird guy smirks. I must've been making a face. I gotta control that.

My mom makes the sign of the cross, "That is horrible," she says, squeamish. Why does everything she says have to contradict me?

"Well, that's where we come in, Arianna," the ginger says. "We're the big dogs that lead the sheep away from the slaughter. Apologies for wearing out that metaphor."

"What is your name, by the way?" Mom asks.

"Oh, where are my manners?" He extends his hand, "Dennis der Teufel."

JJ's brow burrows when Dennis says his name. He shoots him a look.

Does he not trust us?

"Pleasure to meet you, Mr. der Teufel," Mom says as she shakes his hand, "But my son and I aren't looking to be soldiers right now. We are trying to find a place to settle—"

"All the more reason to join my cause," Dennis interrupts. "And please, call me Dennis." I've never seen someone with so much composure and with the ability to silence my mom so easily.

Dennis continues, "I'll show you where you will be settled, as that's where we're going right now. You see, Arianna, us Others as you people call us, we have a civilization that thrives on unity and working together. You put in the work; you reap the reward. It's that simple. And compared to most places out here, besides some in Idaho, this is the best you've got."

"But—" Mom tries saying.

"Let's just see the place," I interrupt.

"Well, we're not going there now," Dennis says. "We'll spend the night here." He slaps the wall of the house, "And tomorrow, we can head over."

My mom's eyes are wild. She looks scared to even step inside the home. However, JJ and Dennis enter without hesitation, walking in perfect stride. I follow, only to be grabbed by Mom.

"What?" I scoff.

"I don't like that man," she says quietly, "he seems oddly familiar and not in a good way."

"It's probably nothing. You're probably just being paranoid again," I break her grip and walk toward the house.

"Hey," she yells, "Mark!" She storms over and stops me from walking in.

"What? I'm trying to go inside," I snap.

"What's gotten into you?" she asks, her big eyes filled with worry.

"Nothing," I say quickly, "Can I go now?"

"Ever since we've left the Paradise City—"

"You mean ever since you left dad behind!" I didn't want to yell about this, especially in front of JJ, but she's not really giving me a choice now.

Her face freezes with shock.

"What?" I continue. "I mean, what'd you expect. Me to be okay with what happened back there? You didn't even try to fight for him."

"Mark, it's not like we had a choice, *mijo*," she pleads.

"Whatever," I push past her. "And I told you to stop calling me that!" *Mijo, mijo, mijo. I'm not five years old anymore. She doesn't need to keep calling me these baby names.* As I enter the house, I pop my head out the door to see her crying. *Yeah, this is my fault.*

"Mom," I say, "C'mon. Let's get some rest, and we can figure things out tomorrow, okay?"

She turns to me and wipes her nose on her sleeve. Walking over, she says, "I didn't want to leave him."

"I know," I say, meeting her halfway, "I'm sorry for saying that." She hugs me, and I hug her back.

I catch Dennis looking at us through a broken window. His bluish eyes scan us. He almost looks worried. *What is it with that guy and staring?*

This whole thing, working with Javier freaking Jones, fighting to make a difference, make a real impact ... it's too enticing. It's like a dream come true. Then we won't have to suffer, stuck in this rut. Mom and I, we'll finally make it good. Live comfortably. I hope she sees it like that. I hope she joins me and becomes one of the big dogs.

CHAPTER 23

NO BETTER TIME THAN NOW

—

JAVIER JONES
DECEMBER 27, 2064

She's here. What's her name? God, why can't I remember her name? She's now dressed in her elephant pj's. Her black hair is tied in a bun. Her olive skin makes the pink pop even more on her pj's. Her green eyes study her holographic notebook, which floats above our bed.

"What are you reading?" I ask unwillingly. By now, it's commonplace for me not to control my words. It's like watching my life on a movie screen. It's exhilarating.

Her sparkling green eyes don't look up from her notebook. She's frowning.

What'd I do now?

"So ... you're still mad?"

She purses her lips and nods.

"Listen, I didn't want to ignore you, but this whole 'advice' thing just isn't working. I'm sorry, but it's not."

Still no response. "Fine, be that way!"

Wait, why are we fighting? I don't want this! Fix it, dumbass! Whatever it is, fix it!

Still reading her notebook, she answers, "You had the chance to do something good, and you stopped because …"

"I was scared! I didn't want to piss off Levi—"

"How many times do I have to tell you? He doesn't care about you! He never has! He doesn't care about any of us! And now you're choosing him over me? In public too to make things worse."

"I'm sorry, but I don't know why I did it. I can't, for the life of me, understand a single reason why I would do something like that."

Like what? Whatever mistake I made, fix it! Just apologize, fool!

Silence consumes the room. She's now lying back on the bed, staring at me, waiting for an answer. I don't have anything to say.

"Are you even going to try to fix this?" she asks, her tone increasing in belligerence. "Because there's no better time than now."

My body is heavy. The guilt is crushing me. Whatever I did, I have to fix it. I have to make things right. "All right," I answer. "How do I fix my mess?"

With a jolt, I wake. Leo is shaking me. His pale block head is hard to look at, especially after looking at that woman.

"What the hell—"

"Shhhh!" Leo shushes. He points over to the door. Mark's standing by the open door, shaking his legs in anticipation. His mom sleeps, still wrapped in a blanket. "Let's go outside," Leo whispers. I get up and sneak around Arianna to the front door. Leo closes it quietly.

Why do I keep dreaming of that girl? Who is she?

"Mark, I have just received word of a mission," Leo says with a thick layer of enthusiasm, "We are going to evacuate a group of people whose home is about to be destroyed by the Wright Gang."

"Who?" he asks, still confused. He keeps shooting me a look. It's like he's worried I might run away from him. "Bad people," Leo says in stride. Despite the warm night, the kid shakes. His athletic build rattles like a leaf on a tree. "And it's tonight," he says as he loads the Grim Reaper into the driver's seat of the pickup.

Mark gives me a puppy dog sad face before turning back to Leo, "What about my mom? She should probably come too. Right?"

"She made it clear she doesn't want to fight," Leo says as he enters the pickup.

Mark is clearly uncomfortable with this. He keeps looking back at the broken home then back to me.

"But we can use all the help we can get, can't we?" I ask Leo for the kid's sake.

"JJ, you can't force someone to do something they aren't willing to do," Leo answers. "They won't give it their all and, in what we are dealing with out here, that can lead to us getting hurt."

"This is wrong," I say, though my gut's not with me on this one. Leo's right. She made it clear she doesn't want to come. But we can't make Mark come either.

Should we really be separating the kid from his mom?

"*There's no better time than now*," the woman's voice repeats in my head. Right. No mistakes. No failures. If I am doing good, do it now.

"There's no better time than now to start helping people," I say to Mark. He looks at me with his big brown eyes and nods, "If you want to stay behind with your mom, that's fine. But understand that if you want to help people, you have to start at some point. Why not now?

Leo grins at this, then hides it almost immediately, "Let's go. We can't afford to be late."

Mark exhales deeply. Taking a look back at the house, he says, "I'm coming back to you, I promise," then heads for the pickup. I join him and slide Leo into the middle seat. Mark's eyes are wild, like a crazed animal.

"You look scared," Leo tells Mark.

"I'm not scared. I've been in plenty of fights before. I can handle myself," he retaliates.

"Good," Leo continues. "Fear is weakness in their eyes. It's their equivalent of sharks smelling blood in the water. One ounce of fear, and they'll destroy—"

"Where is this place?" I interrupt Leo. I get it, scare the kid so that he's not overconfident, but don't make him shit his pants.

"The apartments dead ahead," he responds, a bit disappointed, "They should be arriving soon."

"They? How many are we expecting?" I ask. Leo doesn't respond, his eyes looking up into the sky as if waiting for something to fall from it. "Do we at least have a plan?" I ask.

"Who needs a plan!" Mark yells. "Let's ride!"

I look at Leo, who is equally stunned by Mark's sudden shift to arrogance. He's psyching himself up, bouncing his head to his go-to earworm. Huh, just like I used to do. A slight smile grows on my face.

"What's your ear warm?" I ask the kid.

"'Not for the Faint of Heart' by X."

"X? You don't look like the typical X fan. Where's your jet-black hair and green lipstick?" He pats his pant pockets and looks around. "Oh crap! I left them at home!" he says sarcastically.

"What got you into this type of music anyway?" I ask through my laugh. "I used to listen to her before my football—"

"For the plan," Leo interrupts, agitated by our side conversation, "I'll tell you on the way. We don't want to be late."

What's got his goat?

I slam my foot on the pedal and speed off into the night. In the backseat, Mark cranks his neck, looking back at his mom. "Hey," I say to him. He turns around. The joy that came from his earworm is gone. His skin is green.

"Don't worry about her. We'll be back before she even wakes up. And listen, I went into my first fight with no experience whatsoever. From what you said on the drive up here, at least you played war games. Maybe that'll give you something." He gives a hollow smile.

"I hope so." *What would a general say to get his soldiers pumping?* "Chin up, soldier!" I yell back to him. He hesitantly straightens his back, then over exaggerates his posture. His chin raised high as the ceiling. We both laugh and even Leo cracks a smile.

Yeah, this group is going to have a lot of fun together.

CHAPTER 24

THE WRIGHT GANG

MARK MORALES
DECEMBER 27, 2064

The truck's silent as we close in on the apartments. It's an ancient-looking thing. The truck is jet black, bulky with cut features, and has a short, stubby hood. It's raised about a foot with a V-shaped bottom. And weirdest of all: it's got a steering wheel. How the hell are we supposed to kick any ass when one of us has to actually drive this damn thing?

Dennis's simple plan of "get into an apartment, find their leader, and help any way we can," makes sense. But are we … no. We have a cyborg super athlete on our team. What do they have that can match that?

JJ drives into the apartment complex. The skyscraping four apartment buildings surround a circular grassy parking lot in the center. In the middle is a smaller building. No people are on the ground. There are a couple of cars in the parking lot, but no one in them. A flare is sent up in the distance behind me. Its light reflected in the windshield.

There must be at least a hundred people lined up on the balconies. Some smoke, others drink and laugh. Few are armed.

A lot of the lights in the building are off. It looks like a ghost town.

"Hey Dennis," I ask, "these people know they're about to be attacked, right?"

He doesn't answer me. He just looks up in the black night sky with his brow scrunched together.

JJ parks the trucks with a silent screech. He grabs his rifle from his lap. His eyes looking through the window into the empty square. There's a heavy silence in the night. My chest clenches. My heart is in my mouth. No stars are in the sky. There's no moon. The only light comes from our headlights and a few sky-high apartments.

I've gotta calm down.

The orange flair is still in the air. In the rearview mirror, it looks like it's flying toward us and getting bigger.

"JJ," I'm able to squeak.

He's barely able to turn around before the fiery missile flies overhead. A loud explosion rocks the apartment building next to us. Rubble rains from the sky as the building creaks and groans. Another fiery streak slams into the same building, sending more rubble into the air.

JJ reverses quickly, and the truck jerks back. The momentum forces my body down, slamming my head into the dashboard. JJ drives the truck like a mad man, dodging chunks of building while driving in reverse. The tires squeal as they burn under the vicious turns. But instead of driving away from the scene, JJ drives toward it. His eyes are intently focused on the next building. He continues to dodge collapsing rubble like a running back, finding his gap. Although I'm not sure of it, Dennis seems to smile at this chaos.

"We've seen enough, JJ," Dennis yells over the gunfire, "There's no way anyone here can win this fight. We have to leave now before we die with them."

"That's only one building," JJ yells back. "There's still three more standing."

As the apartment building falls to the ground, JJ makes a U-turn and spins the truck around. But as we round the corner of a building, we see a horde of giant, muscular men dressed in all white clothes standing next to a tank. Before we can even move, a barrage of bullets flies at us, cracking our windshield. I duck my head in between my legs to hide from the bullets.

Although I can't see what's happening, more bullets spray into our truck. A flash in the night sky, then another fiery missile streaks into the building next to us. Chunks of rubble rain down on our truck. JJ does his best, but the increasing amount of building debris continues to dent the hood of the car.

Another flash and more fiery streaks. The third building is taken out by the attackers.

"JJ!" Dennis yells, "Leave now!" We've got no shot here!" Dennis's smile is long gone, replaced with wide eyes and heavy, short breaths.

"One person!" JJ yells back, "I need to save one person."

"What?" I scream back, "What the hell's gotten into you? Let's go before you get us all killed!"

JJ ignores our begging and rounds another corner. Bullets hit the truck again, but JJ refuses to turn away. Instead, he grabs his rifle and tells Dennis, "Hold this," as he lets go of the wheel. Dennis jumps on it, scared. His wide eyes like that of a puppy. Rolling down the window, JJ points his rifle at the tank shooting missiles. He shoots a green laser at the tank. When it hits, the tank explodes, taking out a large number of attackers.

He comes back inside the car and takes the wheel. Dennis has taken us back to the center of the complex. Fire burning on the collapsed buildings lights the battle scene. Hundreds of men in all-white clothes kill everyone in sight. The Others don't stand a chance as the cheering men cut them down with axes, shotguns, and knives. Some team up, beating some of the Others to death.

Instead of driving away or at least through the crowd, JJ parks the truck next to the small building in the middle of the circle. He slaps his head in frustration and says, "Don't go red," then exits the car. Two attackers carrying battle axes smile when they see JJ exit the car. He quickly shoots them down with his rifle.

Be a man. Don't be a coward. There's a reason we left Mom behind. She can't handle stuff like this. I can.

I open the door and jump out. Dennis yells something, but I can't hear him over the gunfire and screams. Picking up a gun from a dead guy, I'm immediately met with the largest man I've ever seen. He holds some sort of electrified spear. He swings it at my head. I dive to the floor. Next to me, a woman with her face bashed in. My eyes water. I can't do this. I can't do this. My face must be hilarious because the man with the spear laughs. He raises his weapon to deliver the final blow. *No. I have to move! Move idiot!* The giant is shot through the back.

"If you're going to die, stay in the car!" JJ yells at me. He shoots down two more before getting pummeled with a rock. A group of attackers runs at him.

My heart pounds so hard I can hear it. My throat closes. I can barely move.

Oh shit. I've gotta ...

I run toward the nearest apartment building. Jumping over corpses and dodging random fighters, I avoid any of the giant muscular men. Out of the corner of my eye, a blinding light flashes. An explosion rocks the apartment building. The building aces and creaks as rubble falls from the sky, crushing some Others and attackers alike.

There's only one building left. I take off and run toward it. Behind me, I can hear people scream as chunks of building fall onto them.

What the hell did I get myself into?

As I approach the building, I look up into the sky. There are no missiles flying toward me now. I just need to hide.

The door of the building is already open. Inside, all the lights are off. The fire light from outside seeps through the cracks in the walls, lighting up the dust in the air. The sound of screams and gunfire are muffled as the door closes behind me.

I can't control my breathing. Each inhale turns closer to a full-fledged gasp. My heart is beating so fast I can feel it through my chest. I can fill it pulsing in my aching head.

Please, no one be in here.

The lobby is empty except for a swinging, broken ceiling light. Its creaks, echoing through the building. To my left is a long narrow hallway. Gunfire goes off above me. My entire body tingles. The muscle in my legs twitching. My vision blurred.

Stay cool. JJ said save one person. I can do that. Grab anyone and run for the truck.

I walk down the hallway. Besides the muffled gunfire from outside and my heavy breathing, the apartment is silent. The dust clings to my sweaty skin. Each door is sealed shut. *What if someone's there? I should check, right?* As I approach the door, my cold feet win, and I just move farther down the hallway.

To my left, one door opens and closes on its own. Its eerie creaking sends a chill down my spine. There's definitely someone inside. Pointing the gun at the door, I walk toward it. My legs shake too violently for me to walk in a straight line. I can't calm my hands. The sight on the pistol is visibly wobbly.

There's a creak behind me. I turn around and shoot. The bang echoes throughout the apartment. It's JJ. He stares at me with bug eyes. An inch away from his foot, a hole in the floor. "You find anyone?" he asks.

As soon as I realize it's him, my body relaxes. I'm no longer alone. "Not yet," I say with a sudden rush of confidence.

"All right, let's—"

"Hey!" a barreling voice yells behind us. A large Arab or Mexican-looking man and another shorter one with the same complexion run up to us.

The large man says in his extremely deep voice, "You leaving?"

"Yeah," JJ says. "Is there anyone else?"

What the hell is he doing? I thought just one.

"Yeah," says the large man. "Joanne came down here before us. Did you see her, a smallish Hispanic lookin' lady? Green hair? Nose ring?"

"No," JJ says as he scouts the outdoors, "but we can look for her. See that truck over there," he points to our truck, "try grabbing as many people as you can and get into the back seat of the truck."

The men nod. The big one whispers something to the normal-sized one. A thud echoes at the doorframe. A small sphere rolls into the room, hissing. As the two men stare at it,

JJ tackles me to the ground. The grenade explodes, lighting the room on fire.

My ears ring. Vision's blurred. Headaches. A heavy object lies on top of me. As my vision clears, it's JJ. He's motionless, his hair smoking. "JJ," I try to say. He doesn't move. I push him off me and roll him on his back. His eyes are open, but he's not blinking. Blood trickles from his head. *He can't be dead.* "JJ," I say as I slap him, "Hey! Wake up!" he doesn't budge.

This is my fault. I should've just stayed in the car. I should—

There's a tug on my shoulder. I grab my pistol and shoot. The normal-sized man from earlier stands behind me. His eyes are wide. His hands covering the blood that pours from his gut. He collapses to the floor, his throat gurgling.

I can't—why did he—

"Hey," JJ's voice brings me back to earth. "Whe—"

"We have to go," I say. Tears puddle in my ears. *Hold them back. Don't be weak.* I pull JJ up off the ground and wrap his arm around me. His feet drag on the ground as I pull him out of the building.

"Gun," JJ whimpers.

"What?" He points to his rifle in the doorway. Squatting, I pick up the gun.

Outside, the battle is still raging on. The attackers are finishing off the last of the Others. They are no longer using their guns, only melee weapons.

Our truck is only around fifty feet away. Dennis is now outside. He tries fighting off a couple of the attackers with a pipe, but they just overpower him. As he swings the pipe, one catches it and rips it out of his hand. Another grabs his arm while another pulls his other arm. The attacker with Dennis's own pipe swings it, breaking Dennis's right arm clean off.

Although Dennis screams, no blood comes from his arm. Instead, it's just wiring. The attackers look at him, confused.

What the hell? Dennis's a Replacement?

"Give me the gun," JJ whimpers.

"What? You can't hit him from this far away." JJ doesn't ask again. With his free arm, he snatches the rifle out of my hand. His eyes glaze over red.

With his one arm free, he points his rifle at the attackers, who are now preparing to rip off Dennis's other arm. JJ shoots his three shots; all go through the head of the attackers. Dennis drops to the ground with a thud.

"Let's go," JJ mumbles. His voice is dry and calm. Face emotionless, yet radiates anger. Blood trickles down his cheek. His eyes burning red.

I drag him toward the car. Without hesitation, JJ shoots down anyone, Other or not, that runs in our way. With his red eyes and blank stare, he looks nothing like himself. He's merciless, showing no remorse for anyone he kills. His face, stone-cold yet sending chills down my spine. All my instincts telling me to run.

I help JJ into the truck. Dennis lies against the front wheel. Fried wiring spills out of his shoulder.

"Stop staring," he whines. He picks his arm up off the road and gets into the truck. I follow, tripping over my own feet as I fall into the backseat.

JJ reverses the truck, leaving behind the Others' camp. The victorious howls of the attackers echo into the night, accompanied by the dissipating sound of gunfire.

In the distance, a motorcycle pursues us. I cannot see who is on it, and I don't want to know.

"JJ, there's—" His eyes are focused on the ground in front of us. His knuckles are white on the steering wheel. His mouth contorted and twisted. He screams, letting out a roar so loud it makes my ears ring. He punches the ceiling of the truck, denting the metal. Veins pop out of his neck and head.

In the corner of my eye, I can see Dennis smirk as he reattaches his arm.

JJ slams on the gas, leaving this massacre behind.

CHAPTER 25

WHY ARE SMART PEOPLE SO DUMB?

ALI SCHOLTZ
DECEMBER 28, 2064

 The sunrise is always the best part of the day. The bottom of the sky is orange, while the top is blue. They shouldn't really mix, but they look so pretty together.

 Janet still sleeps in the seat next to me. She's bundled up in a little ball. Her long hair sticks to anything within reach. The ice burn on her neck is already healing. She wears a large black hoodie she stole from the Wrights. For people that say, "White is right," they have a lot of black hoodies.

 I don't think Charlie will forgive me. He always said I was dumb. I guess I just proved him right.

 The neighborhood we drive through is filled with people. A large river flows on our right side. People fish in it and swim. On the left, there's a bunch of freshly painted houses. They're brightly colored, all neon shades of pink, red, purple, orange. It honestly looks like they just threw up a rainbow. With the sunrise lighting up the river orange, this looks like a video from before I was born.

Levi's sparkly purple sports car really fits in well here. The steering wheel and the dashboard have so many buttons and levers on them. I have no idea what they do. The only one I know is good is "Start." Other than that, the rest looks like a rocket ship.

"Help!" a tall woman in a big brown jacket yells at the edge of the town. She runs into the middle of the road, waving her hands. I have to slam on the brakes so I don't run her over. Janet flies forward and wakes up, obviously happy with the gentle wake up.

"What the hell?" she groans.

"Help me, please!" the woman yells, "They took my son!"

"Ali, just go around her," Janet says, her voice groggy.

No one else gets hurt today. I step out of the car and sling my backpack on.

"No, Ali, what're you doing? Ali!"

The woman smiles in relief and runs toward me. "Thank you, thank you!"

"Where'd they take him?" I ask. Janet slams the door of the car and walks over to us. Her eyes are still half-closed from her rude awakening. Under the hood of the car, Levi bangs his fist and yells something I can't hear.

Janet kicks the car and grumbles, "Shut up," without missing a step.

Why is she so mean to him?

"They went that way," the woman points back toward the rainbow houses. "It was these men dressed in all black." The woman gives Janet a side-eye, "You're not one of them, are you?"

"Who?" she answers.

"No, she's not," I answer for her. "How many men?"

"Only four, I think," the woman takes my hand.

"Please go immediately. They're not too far away." She keeps glancing at the black box tattoo on my wrist. The worry drains from her eyes.

She recognizes the coyote logo. Nice! We're famous!

"We'll be back in a snap, ma'am."

Okay, four guys in black? That definitely sounds like Rat Hunters. Although I don't know why they would be out here. It's kinda far from their territory.

Levi pounds on the trunk of his car. His muffled yelling … is he okay in there?

"What is with you and calling women, ma'am?" Janet asks.

"Uh … I don't know. It seems polite."

"Well, it makes us feel old."

"Oh … sorry, I didn't know."

"Why are you doing this?" Janet asks as she trails behind me.

Oh crap! I forgot my gun! Ah well, hand to hand will make it fairer.

"Because I need to," I say without looking back. "She needed help, and I gave her that help."

"And also left her alone with the most hated man in the world."

Do you think? No … definitely not.

I slide in between a white house and a peach one. Smoke grenade in hand, I scout for anyone. This area is empty.

Great. Not here.

We walk over to the next house. This one is a bright yellow. Peeking through the window, all the lights are off. All I see is my own rugged expression.

I need to shower.

"She did say they went this way, right?" I ask Janet.

"Yup," she says dismissively.

She can at least act interested.

As we move over to the next house, a large explosion shakes the neighborhood. Behind us, a small mushroom cloud floats into the air.

Ah, man. They're over there?

We run into the street. All the people in the small town are on the river, looking back at the fire that now engulfs their town. I sprint over to the scene. Janet follows.

As we get closer, we see what caused the whole commotion. Levi is out of the car. His eyes are crazed like a madman. The woman who begged for my help lies collapsed on the concrete. Her leg is in a not-so-good position.

Another man runs at Levi, who I now notice is bleeding through his shirt. Levi rubs his finger across the hood of the car. As the man gets closer, a machine gun extends from the hood and tears the man in half.

"What are you doing!" I yell at him. I sprint up to him, only for Levi to turn the car's weapons on me.

I freeze in my tracks, hands raised. His bugged-out eyes are tainted red with tiny little red rivers streaking across the whites of his eye. Next to him lie two dead bodies. There's a short and stocky woman with bright pink hair, her body torn in half from the machine guns in this car. Another woman lies on top of her, her head now a pile of mush.

Is he worth this? Should I take him down? Bring him back to Charlie as a reward instead of a helper?

"You are a naïve little fuck, aren't you?" he growls.

"What?"

"'What?' Don't what me!" his voice switches to a high-pitched squeal. "Oh, help me please, total stranger who drives a pretty car. You're my only hope!" he returns to his normal growl. "It's the oldest trick in the book!"

"There's a book?" I ask.

"No!" he interrupts, his palm sliding down his sharp-cut white features. "If these two dumbasses," he kicks one of the dead guys that lie next to his feet, "hadn't accidentally opened the trunk, they would've blown us all to a sky-high living fucking hell!"

He might be beyond help. There's no sadness in him. Only panic.

"But why'd you kill them?" Janet asks. She walks closer to Levi, who quickly turns the guns of the car onto her.

"If you couldn't tell," he says, grinding his teeth, "they were trying to cut me open and paint their street." He points to a small cut on his collarbone. It's not deep, and there isn't too much blood.

"That would've been nice," she mutters.

"Excuse me?" he yells back.

As they continue to argue, the fire from the nearest house grows. A thick black cloud fills the sky, blocking out the sunrise. The people who were on the river are nowhere to be seen.

This is exactly what Charlie didn't want to happen. We're becoming the bad guys. "Hey!" I scream at the two of them. "What the hell are we doing here?" They both stare at me blankly. *For supposedly smarter people than us, these two sure are pretty dumb.*

I continue, "We're supposed to be helping people, not blowing up their towns. That's what we do." I turn to Levi, his jaw still clenched, eyes darting, focusing a single moment on each thing around him. "I rescued you because I thought you could help me save my camp. I thought you wanted to be better than what they say you are. When I saw you on that train, for a moment I thought you were different than the rest of them. Don't prove me wrong."

Levi focuses on me. His eyes lose a hint of their wildness.

I like this! It feels good to assert myself.

"Ali," Janet says softly. "We all feel your pain. Trust me, me more than anyone else, but we can't help people with him around."

"You're right," Levi says.

"He's despicable," she continues.

"True," he responds.

"Disgraceful."

"Yup."

"And just a selfish and shallow person."

"Ooh, there it is!" Levi taunts. "And tell me, what have you done?" The guns fall back into the car.

That's a good step one.

Janet walks up to Levi, getting face-to-face with him. "Saving your dumbass."

"You sure? PC trash like you don't usually do much saving." Janet's confidence shrinks when he calls her PC trash.

"Plus," he mocks, "sure looks like your boyfriend there is doing all the saving."

"He's not my boyfriend," she says, blushing, "We literally just met."

"Right," he says, turning his attention to me. He gives me a look like, "Really?"

Boyfriend? Me and Janet? Can that—no Ali, focus.

He pushes past Janet and walks over to me. He continues, "You just met me, and now here you are preaching, 'Help everyone! Even the ones who stab me.' Look, kid, you can't expect total strangers to work together and be all happy go lucky as you. And from what I've seen, I don't think anyone can."

"Oh, will you just shut up?" Janet interrupts. The hatred behind her voice, it's worse than when we were chased by those assassins. Why does she hate him so much?

"No, keep interrupting me," he quickly strikes back. "Please, it's great to know my life has been ruined by a trashy and spoiled brat from a PC and a pure bread dumbass."

"Look, Levi," I say calmly. *Talking to him is like talking to a tweaker. Calm. Nothing but calm.* "You have all the resources and brains anyone can ask for. The reason I went to get you was because I thought you could help me save my family. It's my goal to just ... be better, I guess. I just want to make sure every person at least has a chance at living a happy life.

"And we don't have to be friends either," I quickly add. "We just have to, I don't know, work together, I guess. For Other's sake. And maybe we won't do something like this again."

Levi looks around at the burning town and the dead bodies. His clenched jaw finally relaxed as he looks at the carnage he's committed.

After a moment of silence, he says, "The Good Life."

I don't get it. Is this another one of his insults?

"What? Isn't that G.L.E.'s motto?" Janet asks.

"It's what I named the car," he says sheepishly. Janet snickers.

"You named your car after a monopoly's slogan?" she antagonizes, holding back a sinister laugh.

What's gotten into her?

"No," he says fully serious. "It's an idea I've had for a while." He pauses for a second, looking up at the sky, then says, "You should've seen the last one I had. Baby Bertha. Damn, she was a beauty. I used to take my son and my wife to the slopes in the Dome, which is this big four sector park in the center of PC:NY—"

"We're familiar," Janet interrupts. It must be the light, but a tear drips down his muddy and greasy face.

Wait, used to ... wife and son? Oh ...

Janet must see this too. Her body finally relaxes. All this anger in both of them, its really hurting us. He obviously has had one horrible life. But Charlie said that Levi was rich and happy working with Marshall? Why would Marshall get rid of Levi and take him away from his family?

Levi's paralyzed body stiffens. His hands clenched in fists. Blood drips from them as his nails dig into his palms. "I have to get back," he mumbles under a sob. "I have to see you again."

Who is he talking to? Does he have one of those brain chips with his family? Is he seeing them now?

"Two rules only," he says, interrupting my questions. "I drive everywhere," he takes the keys out of my hand, "and you have to stop falling for the dumbest traps."

"That sounds easy enough," I say, squealing in delight. Do I tell him my name? There was a reason Charlie always said no. But I think I have to. Maybe he'll do "dumbass decisions" for us then. "Oh, I'm Ali, by the way. And that's Janet," I say nervously.

"Yeah, so you've said," he says quietly. Now that I'm closer to his face, I can see him more clearly. "So," he says, walking back to the car, "where's this camp of yours?" He and Janet both look at me.

Why are they looking at me? Oh right! "It's my camp," I say, my voice cracking with excitement. Levi pulls out some gauze from inside the car and wraps his hands and collarbone. I continue, "All we have to do is go in and get rid of this Dennis guy—"

"He means Leo," Janet interrupts.

Who's Leo?

Levi freezes mid-wrap. "Leo Santos?" he asks, his voice frail.

"Yeah," Janet asks, her voice wavering.

"Why does that scare you so much?" His body hasn't moved since freezing. His eyes locked on the floor. His already pale face turning a lighter shade of white. "If he's at your camp, kid, there's a good shot they're, uh ... you know."

He doesn't know that. They're not ... He's just scared. That's all. He's—

"Well, we better hurry before it's too late," I enter the car, and he does too.

"Great," he says as he enters the Good Life. A strained smile fights its way onto his face. Something got him happy.

I gotta figure out what that is, "Girl, you're in the back this time."

"My name's Janet," Janet scoffs, "and why do I have to get in the back?"

"Because you're the smallest, and if you're lucky," he looks back at her and smiles, "you get to operate the big gun."

Big gun? Wow, he needs a lot of work.

I get in the Good Life with my new team. Levi completes the bandage around the small knife wound on his shoulder. Getting a closer look at him, I can see all his scars. In his thick brown hair is a bald spot. It's on the back of the head. Stitches sloppily hold together the thick wound. In his black Wright Gang shirt, he looks like someone I would've knocked out if I didn't know who he was.

In the back, Janet still sits pretty. Although she's hunched because she's too tall for the back seat, she still looks beautiful in her dust-covered crop top. Her wavy reddish brown hair hugs her shoulders. Her green eyes catch the light, giving them a twinkle.

Janet's boyfriend? Huh ...

Levi starts the car and flies off down the river.

CHAPTER 26

RIVALS, FRIENDS, AND THE P.R.R.C.

JANET SIMS
DECEMBER 28, 2064

Of all the people I wanted here, Levi was not even on the list. I mean, he's just the worst. He got rich off other people's suffering. He *literally* divided us and designed so much oppression it's unbelievable. He is right about one thing; Ali is really naïve. I honestly don't get how he's lived this long. I mean, trust a guy like Levi, a narcissistic, controlling, and overall asswipe, I don't get it. Now he has me scrunched up in the back of a two-seater car. I can barely get my body to squeeze in here. My knees are in my chest, and my head bangs into the ceiling with each bump in the road.

"Where exactly are we going?" Levi asks. Even his voice is annoying. He sounds like he has the flu.

"An apartment complex a couple of miles past the Funstein Trading Mile," Ali says as he drums his legs. He's antsy. His smile cannot be contained, his eyes excited like a kid on Christmas. His leg bounces up and down with nervous energy.

"You have a trading system out here?" Levi asks way too enthusiastically. "That's fascinating. Did you create a civilization too? Or is it more an anarchic system?"

"A what?" Ali asks.

"Really, Levi?" I interrupt before he can ask another stupid question. "He's not a science experiment."

"I know," he says, "I'm genuinely curious how—"

"He lives in this world you created?"

Levi flips a switch on the steering wheel and looks at me. He's old. I never noticed it before, but getting a closer look at his pale face, he's really old. He has wrinkles lining his sharply-cut features, his thick brown hair is filled with tiny gray specks. And it's hard to imagine, but he has smiling wrinkles.

"This was never my intention," he adds, his frail voice scratching against his dehydrated throat. "I wanted to create a special place, a safe haven for us to live in while the P.R.R.C. attempted to colonize us. Marshall told me that he would initially open up the city to the best and brightest so that it can be prepared for …"

"The Others," I scorn, "the people you left behind to rot as slaves and die in this apocalypse while you fat cats got rich."

"Yeah," he says helpless, damn near defenseless, "All my life, I've been trying to avoid my mistakes. I hid from it. I took the blame. But then … my family," he chokes up. His eyes water, "I have to avenge the people I've failed. I have to get them to their good life, whatever that may be because I stopped them from getting it. It's the only way to see them again."

What does he mean, "see them again?" Where'd they go?

"We're here!" Ali exclaims. White smoke flows into the sky. As we turn into a circular designed apartment complex … it's gone. All of it. The four buildings, that prison I was in.

All that's left is the tiny office in the center of the circle. Fire burns on some of the rubble. Guns, knives, and spears lie out on the red-tinted pavement. Not a body is in sight.

Ali ...

He's frozen. Sitting in the Good Life. He hasn't blinked, his jaw on the floor. Levi exits the car. He examines one of the weapons on the ground. Ali bolts from the car. He runs into the small office in the center.

"Ali!" I yell as I chase after him. My first step out of the Good Life lands with a pop. A warm liquid drips down my leg. *Please don't be blood.* My white clothes are now a dark red. *Oh, God! Oh, God!* My nerves are on fire. My entire body tingles and twitches. Ali's inside the small office. I need to see if he's okay.

"You said Leo was here," Levi yells from a distance. He's walking toward me, holding an ax the size of his body.

"Um, yeah," my voice is hoarse. I strain my neck just to get the words out. "He locked me in a cage here before Ali saved me."

"He recognized you were PC," Levi expresses in his robotic tone. "Didn't want you blowing his identity. Then when you guys came to rescue me, he probably struck a deal with the Wrights to eliminate this place for betraying them."

"The Wrights?" I ask.

"All you need to know is they're bad news. Animals who thrive on displays of physical power."

"How are you talking about this so casually? All these people are dead, and you're taking it like it's nothing!"

"Desensitization. I've come to expect the worst and only the worst ..." His eyes crunch together. His mouth shrinks and makes an O shape.

What's he doing? Doesn't matter. Go check on Ali.

As I try to leave Levi behind, he follows, now holding a flash drive in his hand. *Where'd he get that from?* He pushes past me and jogs into the small office.

Inside, Ali lies on the floor, his face buried in a picture of a girl his age, with green hair, a nose ring, and a gorgeous complexion. On the bottom is a note written in sloppy cursive reading, "One week til Vegas."

"Who's that?' I ask as I lie down next to him.

"Dr. Jesus," his tone has done a full one-eighty. It's a monotone and empty like he's lost the will to speak.

Levi tries turning on an old computer. It doesn't budge. He bends down and starts fiddling with the wiring below it.

"Was she important to you?" I ask.

"Yeah," he responds, "they all are."

Are? Maybe some escaped.

"Dr. Jesus saved my life, you know," he continues with a small hint of energy. "After my first run, they thought I was done. Couldn't walk again. But she was smart. Smarter than me. She was good with words. Knew a lot of them."

The computer Levi fiddles with turns on, lighting the room white. He plugs in the flash drive, not even paying attention to Ali.

I can't get a read on Ali. He should be in shambles! His entire life has been upended by this Wright Gang! Why isn't he crying? He's sitting there, just ... stoic. Empty.

Maybe he's in denial.

A loud crash from across the room. Levi kicks the computer he tossed on the ground. "Idiots!" he screams, "They're idiots!" He yanks the flash drive from the computer and throws it across the room. I dive to the ground to avoid being hit.

"What the hell are you—" He lies on the floor sobbing. Wailing describes it better. Ali gets up to comfort him.

He's so full of himself he doesn't even care that Ali needs the consoling, not him! What can be so important that it causes that kind of reaction?

"You okay?" Ali says, sitting next to him.

This is wrong. It should be the other way around. He doesn't deserve a pity party.

"They should've gotten me involved," he whines. "Why wouldn't they tell me ..."

"They probably had their reasons," Ali responds kindly. He's still in shock, and now he's found the perfect distraction. Great. This won't come back to haunt him.

Levi looks at me from the ground. "You gonna sit there or come look?"

I approach the computer. On it is a letter from the P.R.R.C., the headline, "We are finished."

"They've been gone for six years. Killed each other because the Russians wouldn't share their crops with the Chinese states. I knew this, and Marshall made me a deal. He told me if I spoke of this to anyone, he would kill me and send my family out here to die. In turn, my family and I got to live in the city where I would be his fall guy. Any mistake in the city, it's my fault. But he didn't keep his promise. I don't know, but Aisling and Kaiya ... they got their hands on this and were about to tell the whole country that their biggest enemy doesn't even exist. And somehow, he learned about it and ..."

He can't finish the sentence. His body shivers.

This can't be true. There's no way something as big as this can't be noticed. Especially with all the information we get? It doesn't make sense ...

"Well, I guess we have a new mission then," Ali's stern voice announces. "We have to break into a Paradise City and tell everyone."

What is wrong with him? Why can't he just focus for a second?

"There's no chance in hell that's happening," Levi responds. "I don't know how you did it before, but there's no way that place is still available."

"You're right, it's gone, but we found another way out," he says, smiling. His eyes are dead. There's no life in them. He's smiling, but there's no joy behind it.

People grieve in different ways. Maybe this is his way.

"Yeah, we used the Dome," my voice frail, "It's not too complicated to get through. Once we do that, we'll be inside the center of the city. Close enough to G.L.E. headquarters to upload this to every device in the city."

"Great, and then I know a guy who can reconstruct our faces, change our eye color, and give us some robotic hands, so we don't have fingerprints," Ali gloats, his enthusiasm slowly coming back.

Wait, this can actually work. We won't be recognized by literally anyone and can secretly end Marshall and G.L.E.

Levi isn't convinced. His head is hung low. His eyes are still red, and his shoulders slouched. He scans our faces. It's like watching an AI trying to learn emotions.

Finally, he sighs, "Fine," and stands. He picks the flash drive off the floor and pockets it.

Ali jumps at Levi and wraps him in a bear hug, almost taking him back down to the floor. "Thank you!" he screams in Levi's ear.

"Okay, thank me when this works," he responds, awkwardly patting Ali on the back. After a brief moment, he pushes Ali off of him. "So," he says, clearly flustered and blushing, "are we ready to, uh—"

"Yeah, we can go," I tease, "Don't worry, you've done enough talking for the day. You've earned a break." Levi mumbles something to himself and exits the small building.

As I follow, there's a pull on my arm. Ali holds it. My look must be more aggressive than I realize because he lets go quickly.

"Thank you," he says softly, his eyes hanging low to the ground.

"For what?"

"For being here for me. For helping me get through this."

"It's what friends are for, right?"

He sinks a bit lower when I say friends.

Oh, is he ...

"Right, anyway, you ready to go overthrow the government?" he's almost back to his excited self. He's smiling that ear-to-ear grin, with that joy in his voice, but he's still hurting. He's putting on a performance, and I don't know why, but as long as it makes him happy.

"Yeah," I smile back, "let's do it."

CHAPTER 27

MOONSHOTS AND OTHER DUMB DREAMS

―

LEVI O'SCANDRICK
DECEMBER 28, 2064

The gentle hum of the Good Life's four battery engines is all that fills the silent drive. The poor kid, his entire family killed by the Wrights. Everyone who comes near me gets hurt. I can't be around anymore. I still have to complete my one good deed, but maybe that's just eliminating myself.

The flash drive feels like dead weight in my pocket. It's horrifying. Something this fragile holds the greatest lie in history. Unite over a common enemy, even after they killed each other.

And Kaiya ... what was she thinking? How did she even get her hands on P.R.R.C. servers? That's the only place this information exists! She must've had help from someone, and that's why ...

"But what about the Wright Gang," Ali blurts out. A shiver goes down my spine. "You want to kill off the Wright Gang?"

"No, of course not," he says. "We don't kill, remember? Look, all we need to do is destroy their base. Then, they'll be running around, trying to find some other place to build their weapons and stuff." His usually perky and twisted eyes that shout, "Imma do something bad and Imma like it!" are now dead. They hold no emotion. They hold no sorrow. They're the eyes of a quitter. The eyes that look too familiar.

Janet is no better. She repeatedly darts her gaze from her lap to Ali. She's wrapped in a tight ball, hugging her knees. Her reddish-brown hair has lost its volume from the days of no treatment. And the best part is ... she couldn't care less. She's changed. Now more worried about Others' sake, particularly one Other, rather than the things she used to put on a pedestal.

The longer they are with me, the more likely they will end up gone. Their future is so bright. I can trust them. Maybe they can right the rest of my wrongs when I'm gone.

I can't let this happen.

"I think breaking into the Paradise Cities is all we need to do. No need to fight a losing battle," I quickly add.

Ali interjects, "But I thought you said—"

"I know what I said!" I shout. Both of them look at me stunned.

Cool it. Be passionate, but don't drive them away.

"I mean, our best option is to go to the Paradise Cities and take our chances there."

"Well, I don't think that'll work, Levi," Ali says. "The Wright Gang is in the Dome's tunnels. We saw them when we escaped. Janet's wanted for murder! If she goes back there, she's dead. I'm a coyote, so they'll just kill me. You're definitely dead because even people out here hate you, and then we're back to ... well ... square zero."

I can blow a hole in the wall with the Good Life, finally, end this whole mess I've made. Restart this world to include everyone, not exclude the unspecialized.

"That doesn't make a difference," I say desperately. "If you ... If we redo our faces, eye color beforehand, then enter the city, and get this information out to everyone, we'll be fine."

But the Pyramid ...

"How about this," Janet says. She puts her hand on my shoulder and continues, "How about we deal with the Wright Gang, destroy one base of theirs, then we can sneak back in *if* all goes well."

"Yeah, but we'll be killed—"

"Not if we do it from a distance," Ali interrupts, a sudden spark in his eye. "Janet and I can sabotage their equipment after you draw them out with the Good Life."

What the hell are they doing? I'm giving them a plan that'll lead them to safety, a better life where they can live in a paradise forever. I'll die doing it, but I've lived a life of regret. I've got no reason to go on.

"Plus," Janet adds, her voice is back to its nasally and energetic tone, "you get to blow up some shit. I know you love to do that."

"A bit too much," Ali complains. He laughs for the first time in hours. Not a typical Ali laugh, but he's getting there.

"I don't get it," I say, baffled. "Don't you guys want to be in paradise? Don't you want to escape this hell?"

"This 'hell' is my home," Ali says with a sudden wave of pride. "And I'll do whatever it takes to make it better. When that's done, then we can go live in your fancy Paradise City."

Butterflies fill my stomach. *Do they know I can't go with them? Is this why they're being so stupid?*

"Fine," I mumble, "but you better get to PC:NY when you're done."

"You mean we," Ali says.

"Sure," I say, ambivalent.

The purple smiling moon flashes before my eyes. My family sits in this world, waiting for me. I have to get there. I have to cross that line.

This feeling is something I don't really know how to describe. It's like I'm eighteen again, moving out of my parents' house to go to college. The butterflies in my stomach aren't scaring me. They're forcing me to smile. To feel like my future is in my control. Right now, a new page of my life has been torn, daring me to write on it.

CHAPTER 28

DUST CLOUDS AND DEMONS

JAVIER JONES
DECEMBER 29, 2064

Sitting alone in a small wooden room, my head aches. The woman hasn't visited me since the incident. It's like she's avoiding me. I can't remember her name. Her face. It's just a blur. *C'mon, this is easy. Remember a face. One face. That's it. The color of her dress: blue. The color of her hair …*

"You ready to talk?" Leo's standing in the doorway. His red hair sticks out in the dark night.

"About what?" I ask. "Where's the kid?"

"He's outside," Leo responds. "You scared him off while you slept. Yelling about some woman."

I did? I didn't even … maybe he knows who she is. "Did I give a hint about who she is? Do you know her?"

Leo scrunches his beady eyes together, "How would I know what goes on in your head, JJ? They're your thoughts. Your memories."

"But you built—"

"We can talk about your dreams some other time," Leo interrupts, his normal monotone now wavery. "Right, now I need you to listen to me." Leo's freckled face looks outside into Nowhere. In the distance, smoke from our fight clouds the sky.

"Is something wrong?" I ask.

Leo leaves the doorframe and sits on the floor next to me. His blue eyes were wide, exuding worry. "What happened back there can't happen again. The Wright Gang ... they're evil, JJ. Marshall's used them for decades. They're like his private army, killing whoever he wants without question. And the worst part is, they enjoy it. Death to them is fun. It's something they joke about."

"If you know this, why didn't you do anything to stop them? If the public found out—"

Leo interrupts, "If I tried to bring him down any other way than what I am doing now with you, I would have failed. Marshall has too many obstacles to disrupt whatever front I attempt to breach. But I'm not here to explain myself to you. I need a favor."

"All right," I respond. "What is it?"

"If I ever get captured by anybody that you think will torture me or use me as bait against you, kill me."

He's kidding, right?

"Leo, your screws must be loose if you think—"

Leo raises his hand, cutting me off, "JJ, it's what I was designed for. When I die, my consciousness gets uploaded into a new body. This one is temporary. Designed to be replaced."

"This is insane!" I scream, "I'm not shooting you."

"JJ, you understand we have to take down the Wright Gang, if not to avenge the Others they killed then for our own clean consciences. For some reason, they're much more organized than before. They actually have a plan of attack rather than just running directly at their enemies and overpowering them. They must have a new leader helping them cleanse Nowhere. If I get captured …"

"I get it. That won't happen, though. I promise."

A loud revving of a motorcycle grows in the distance. A dust cloud plumes in the sky. "We should go," Leo announces, spooked by the cloud.

"Now? What about the kid?"

"Ask him. He'll come. I don't doubt it."

We exit the abandoned house. The Nowhere air is dry, my eyes itch. Mark holds a broken pipe, adamantly starring at the dust cloud. Leo heads straight for our truck. Its windows shattered and cracked. The dented black exterior, stained with blood.

If he hadn't run off and needed saving, then killed someone, maybe I could've actually saved a life. Maybe the Wrights wouldn't have killed everyone. He's reckless. We should've left him with his mom.

"We're going," I tell Mark.

"Yeah, I heard you guys. I'm just worried about my mom."

"You don't have to come if you don't want to," I respond. "I can't force you to do anything you don't want to do. The choice is yours."

The dust cloud grows in the distance. A single rider on a motorcycle drives toward us. "Fine," he says, "I'll go with you."

"Great," I say as I head toward the truck, "and don't worry. We're about to do some real good here. I hope you know that."

"I do," he says as he follows me. "I don't get why we have to fight these guys again."

"Because Mark," I respond as I enter the driver's seat, "there's a certain meanness in this world, and we're apparently the only ones who give a damn."

***

The Wright Gang headquarters is a factory. It's a big brown building with giant brick-colored smokestacks coming out from the top. In the dark night, blanketing this ashy desert, it blends in perfectly. The factory has three entrances, a massive garage door in the front, and two side doors. On the roof, there's a balcony where snipers can easily pick people off.

I park the beaten-up pickup truck at the top of a ledge, about two hundred yards away from the building. Another small ridge rests a bit closer to the factory, a good place for hiding. Behind us, a singular dust cloud continues to follow. *If it's an attack, so be it.* Through the cracked windshield, a small, shiny purple speck comes into view.

It's a sports car. Driven at an insane speed toward the closer ridge. "Is that them?" Mark asks.

"It could be," Leo responds. "They do love overtly offensive cars." The purple sports car pulls to a stop behind the ridge, almost out of sight. I can barely see anything from this distance. As if on cue, my vision zooms in on the area.

That's new.

With a closer look, my heart breaks. Stepping out of the car is a man I thought I'd never see again. *Levi. He's alive? Why is he here? What the hell is going on?* I look at Leo, who is struggling to see the scene.

His words ring in my head, "He betrayed you and his family in order to spare his own life. My boss wanted him dead for a mistake he made, and in turn, he traded your life for his."

"The Wright Gang is very ... Old Testament with their captives."

"They must have a new leader."

Of course.

I slam my hands on the dashboard of the car. How could I be so stupid? He sold me out to live. He was captured by people who wanted to kill him, and now he is selling out everyone to live again. Killing us. He's actively killing people to stay alive.

"What the hell was that?" Mark screams. "Are you all right?"

"You were right," I say to Leo, holding back tears. "I don't know if you led me here on purpose or what, but you were right all along."

Leo stares at me with so much sadness it hurts.

"What do you mean he's right?" Mark asks.

No one responds.

"What's he talking about?" Mark asks again.

"He's here, isn't he?" Leo asks, saddened.

All I can do is nod. *Not another soul. He can't hurt another fucking soul.* I open the door and take out the Grim Reaper. My eyes are in the red tint.

"JJ, wait," Leo pleads. "Wait!"

Putting the gun into sniper configuration, I look down the scope. There are two other people with him—a young man with dark skin, short blond hair, and a goofy smile, and a young, college-aged redhead wearing a white crop top stained with blood, dirt, and ash. That damn ridge is blocking my view of him. He's there, talking to the boy, but I can't see him. The girl ducks behind the ridge and grabs something from the purple car.

I guess he'll do.

I pull the trigger and shoot down the boy, eliminating the first of Levi's "allies."

CHAPTER 29

THE FACTORY PART ONE

LEVI O'SCANDRICK
DECEMBER 29, 2064

It's a beautiful night in the desert. The moonlight reflects off the compressed ash that covers the barren ground. Dead trees and broken homes surround us as we drive off-road to the factory. Some rain has started to fall for the first time in a couple of weeks, turning the ground below us sloshy.

"The worst way to die is when you're lying on your deathbed and, looking back at your life, realizing you lived a life full of regret, and knowing there's nothing you can do to change it."

My dad's words echo to me as Janet and Ali laugh about something I'm not listening to. Is that the code? Is that how I become happy? Get to see my family again? I know I haven't lived the greatest of lives, but each thing I've done has been set on trying to help people. If I can make these two better people, can I even say I've lived a good life?

"You both have to promise me right now," I say firmly, interrupting their conversation. "If things go south here, you two will leave without question, you hear me? No hesitation. No nothing. You're gone."

"You can't think like that," Janet mocks. "Now you're just asking for it."

"You're wrong," I say feverishly. "Life is one big pendulum, and no matter how good things get, it always swings back to bad."

"I don't believe in superstitious things," Ali says.

"I'm serious," I respond. "All my life, that's how it was. I went to the college of my dreams, the world ended. I met the love of my life, my parents died. I take up the most ambitious engineering project in human history, Nowhere, and my family dies because of it."

"I remember reading on Pixie," Janet says, "these wise words from my guru, Andrea Hargobind. She said, 'Life isn't filled with black and white, good and evil. It's a whole lotta gray.' And," she gestures to the gray world around us, "she was right. There's no doubt your life is a spectacular failure, but—"

"Will you promise me you will leave?" I interrupt. My eyes sting as tears puddle. They both actively avoid my gaze. *What have I done to earn this?*

We arrive at the factory. In the moonlight, it looks like something out of a cheesy horror movie with its rusted and broken appearance.

I park behind a ridge about ninety meters away from the factory, hiding us from being spotted. Ali and Janet both exit the Good Life before me. Ali takes his backpack and places it on the ashy earth. He hands Janet one of his pistols and a couple of extra rounds of darts. The night air is frigid. When I step out of the Good Life, it's a slap in the face.

"What're you doing?" Janet asks me. "You can wish us good luck in the car where it's actually warm."

"I know, but," *am I seriously going to do this? Sure,* "when I was with the Wrights for those three days, I wanted to kill myself. My only goal is to do one good deed, that's it, only one thing that actually makes someone's life better. So I built this car and appropriately named it the Good Life, so when it explodes, I can finally have mine. I would've killed the entire leadership of the Wright Gang and myself, doing my one good deed."

"Wait," Janet interrupts. "You mean we're driving in a bomb!"

"Of all the things to take away from that," I scoff.

"It's kind of an important thing!" she yells as she runs out of the car.

"Well, if it makes you feel better," Ali says, bringing us back to the topic, "you had a big impact on me. When I put that wrapper in your pocket on that train, I saw sadness in you when you were looking out into Nowhere that made me rethink for a moment that all people in Paradise Cities were selfish. I wouldn't have even considered helping Janet if it weren't for that. I don't know if that counts, but that could be your one good deed."

I stare at him dumbfounded, then say, "What is wrong with you?"

"Huh?" he responds elegantly.

"You have every reason in the world to hate me, and you don't because I looked sad out a window?"

"Well yeah," he says with a sly smirk on his face. "And look what it led to!"

"Unbelievable," I say. "I guess I can take that as my one good—"

Ali's face is stone-cold. His eyes frozen. His jaw locked. In his hip is a clean hole. A clear wound cut through his body like a laser. He collapses onto the hood of the Good Life with a hollow thud.

"Ali!" Janet screams.

He puts a thumb in the air and says delightfully, "I'm good! Stay over there. See," he gestures to his legs, "it's nothing."

Janet and I duck behind the Good Life. *Where'd that come from?* It couldn't've been from the factory since we're blocking it, so it must've come from behind. No, the angle was off, but—

"What do you mean 'it's nothing' there's a hole in your—" she stammers. Ali's leg is cut clean through. Instead of blood and flesh, gears and wiring comprise the make of his leg. "You're a—"

"Only half robot," Ali gets out. "Like I said, my first run didn't go so good. Dr. Jesus came up clutch," he winces in pain. "Still hurts, though."

I turn around and see them. A black pickup truck that's in tatters. Standing next to it, a lone gunman that looks oddly familiar. He looks like JJ if he had a beard, was permanently frowning, and had glowing red eyes. Another man walks out of the truck. His skinny frame, the smoothness to his walk, the red hair ...

Leo? Marshall really wants me dead.

But it's just me. Leo will follow only me. Hunt only me. Maybe I can get a two for one on good deeds today. Actually, make it a three for one ...

I pull the flash drive out of my pocket and hand it to Janet. "You two have to leave now."

"What?" Janet protests. "We didn't make any—"

"Janet, those guys up there are after me and me alone. They think I have that flash drive, and they'll do anything, including torturing you both to get it from me." Taking another peek, Leo is focused on me. His beady eyes filled with a sinister delight.

"We're not leaving you, Levi," Ali groans. "I can still help in this car if—"

"Dammit, will you just shut up! You need to get out of here, understand?"

"What?" Janet yells back, "No, I don't think—"

"Don't think about it, just go! And whatever you do, don't let anyone touch this flash drive. You understand? Get it into PC:NY. Follow our plan and tell the world."

Unless the Pyramid—no. Stop thinking like that.

She's crying now, "Levi, I don't want to—"

"Go!"

I throw a black smoke grenade to conceal us. With Janet's help, Ali drags himself into the car. They hide behind the Good Life. Ali climbs over the driver's seat into shotgun. Ali's backpack is on the ground, away from us. I grab a smoke grenade and throw it on the ground, consuming us in a black haze.

"Here!" I run over to Janet and give her the backpack. She takes it and puts it in the back seat.

"Just come with us!" she pleads.

"Janet, I can't. These are people from my past. They are my problem—"

"That's the stupidest thing I've ever heard—"

"They will hunt me and everyone I give a damn about until they're all dead! That means you, that means him, that meant my son and my wife ..." The smoke is beginning to fade. "We don't have time for this," I say.

I push Janet into the driver's seat and slam the Good Life's doors closed. Placing my hand on the car, I lock the door, then say, "Find a workshop beyond ten miles radius from this position. Once there, transfer all ownership to Janet Sims." The Good Life dings in response.

I turn to her and say, "Put your hands on the wheel."

"Just get in the—" Another laser flies at us. This one hits the Good Life's hood and goes clear through.

"I'll find you! Now go!" I yell at her. Janet drives away teary-eyed. The Good Life speeds off deep into Nowhere, far away from the ensuing battle.

I run and dive behind the front of the ridge, where the shooter can't reach me. Looking back at the purple beauty, all I can do is hope they'll get to live a life better than mine.

Now that they're gone, time to do things my way. Next to me, a couple of loose trank darts and one hurt grenade. So, an assault is off. I'm going to have to sneak around. *Great. Now I'm Ali.* How am I going to keep Leo away? I take a quick peek over the ledge. Leo is still standing with his soldier pet, whose barrel is still pointed in my general direction. The black smoke is nearly gone. The closest door is a solid one hundred meters away. *I need time.*

I can't use the grenade cuz I need it to ignite the flame. There's definitely some form of oil in there. It's a factory. And the darts are useless from this distance. Do they even work on cyborgs?

Fuck it. Hopefully, the Wrights see me and swarm out here. And if I get shot, Leo will gloat. Use the grenades to take him out too.

I sprint toward the door. The sparkly ashy ground clouds around me, getting thicker with each step. About halfway, a laser slips past my head, missing me by an inch. The heat from the laser singes some hair.

Now within a couple of meters from the door, the factory creaks and groans as the massive garage door slowly grinds open. Inside, it sounds like hundreds of men are screaming and cheering.

Finally.

I run past the garage, not risking getting spotted. As I enter the factory, another laser shoots through the door, missing me by an inch. The heat of the laser, although not touching me, still burns my arm, turning it red. *Who the hell is this guy?*

Inside the factory, I'm immediately met with my first Wright. He's a big man with large, beefy arms and legs the size of tree trunks. He has a braided beard and red war paint on his face. I stick him in the neck with a dart. The man's eyes glaze over as he collapses. I catch and gently place him on the ground to avoid getting noticed.

As I lower the body, about a hundred Wright Gang members, all fully armed and dressed for battle, hoot and holler as the garage completes its sluggish opening. About ten buggies carrying Wrights in bunches swarm outside like locusts on a humid night. Behind them, an old large, tan tank slowly approaches the now open factory door.

Dammit! How am I supposed to kill them all now?

There's a second-story ring made of wood that circles the inside of the factory. It's incomplete, the far side not connected to anything. A welding torch sits on top of a workbench on the first floor. *All I need is some oil.*

The 'roided up Wrights pay no attention to me. They are too focused on the chaos outside. Leo must've brought backup. There's no way he and that other guy could do this. As the last of them empty out, I sneak behind the tank and grab the welding torch off the bench. The ground rumbles and shakes as the tank rolls forward.

The first floor is filled with half-completed projects. Car frames are scattered aimlessly on the floor, some raised on lifts. Other benches have weapons being developed. Molds of giant axes and gun printers hide in the back. And next to them ...

Hell yeah.

Two beautiful barrels of oil. I sprint over with the torch. The barrels are semi-empty, one at half, and the other at a quarter full. Based on the size of the factory, this won't be enough to destroy the whole thing. But it'll at least start a flame. A wooden staircase to my right leads to the second story. *That'll do.*

The ground stops shaking. The tank has reached the edge of the door and fires its first shot with a loud bang. I drag the first barrel of oil over to the stairs. It spills onto them and the floor beneath. I run back over to get the second barrel. The tank shoots its next shot with a thunderous clap. The barrel's now in position.

I need a fuse. In my vicinity, there's nothing but a long chain, some gloves, and a rusted sword. *I guess that'll work.* I put on the gloves and coat the chain in oil. A fiery explosion shakes the factory. Behind me, the tank is on fire. The wall above it groans in rapid succession as cracks spread through it. It collapses onto the tank.

Well, that helps.

Running back to the length of the fifty-foot chain, I take off the gloves and throw them at the barrel. Laying the chain on the ground, I light it with the torch. It erupts into flames. The fire sprints toward the barrels and explodes, setting the back half of the building on fire.

Step one, done. Now for the extra fun part.

I take the hurt grenade and throw it onto the ceiling, setting it to explode in forty seconds. Sprinting back toward the entrance, the door bursts open. Seven Wrights stand in front of me, baffled their factory is on fire.

I punch one in the nose, then turn to run. One of the other Wrights grabs me and throws me up the staircase. Its fire is burning rapidly. The Wright wraps his hands around my neck, crushing my windpipe. Slapping my hand around my hip, I finally find a dart. I stab the Wright in the neck with it. His eyes glaze over, and he falls off of me. The other six now chase me. As I'm about to run, the door opens again. It's Leo's shooter, accompanied by a much younger soldier. He looks at me, his eyes glowing red.

Of course, they are.

He looks so familiar.

I sprint away from the Wrights toward the fire. Looking up at the hurt, the red numbers read, "twelve." The Wrights chase with their melee weapons. Gunfire follows.

I don't look back as the hurt explodes. I jump through a window, glass cutting my face and arm as I fall into the cold night. I land not so gracefully on my legs and roll before slamming into a small ridge. With blurred vision, I can't see what's happening around me. My head rings, probably another concussion. As my vision clears, my leg looks like it's been torn apart. Blood soaks through my torn pants with shards of glass sticking out.

The heat from the burning factory singes the hairs on the back of my neck. I did it. I'm done. My good deed is done. The Wrights have been handled or at least slowed down. I wonder where Janet and Ali are now. I get up from the gray, ashy dirt and walk away from the burning factory.

Why did that man look so familiar?

"You surprise me, Levi." That sharp sting of Leo's voice shakes me. "You're presented with an opportunity to do some good, and then you burn it down." He stands on top of a small rise above me, looking down at my broken body like he's the king of Rome.

"How did I not know it was you earlier," I tease.

"People see only what they want to see—"

"Oh, don't feed me more of your "wise words," you ignorant jackass. They're about as deep as a freshly dried puddle."

Leo smirks, "JJ doesn't think so."

My body shivers as he says that name. That man …

I look back at the factory. JJ's standing on a balcony as the factory burns. He doesn't look anything like the man I knew. He's hunched over, has an untamed beard, wild-man hair to his shoulders.

"So, do you want to kill him, or should I?" Leo taunts.

I run at Leo with a new wave of energy. He dodges my first attack with ease. I swing again but miss. He's like an orca, playing with his food before he kills me. I can barely put any weight on my leg. My cut body shivers in the cold night. Leo punches me in the mouth, knocking me back. *Get him with the dart.* I stand up and get ready to swing again. He runs at me. Using his momentum against him, I dodge his attack like a matador and stick the dart in the back of Leo's neck. He crumbles to the floor with a satisfying heap. My leg is weak. The muscles barely obey my commands.

Back on the balcony, JJ now stares at me. He jumps down back on the ground, shooting a couple of Wrights when he lands.

What did he do to you?

I've got to break him out of it. There's got to be a way to do that. Home. I can take him home. Maybe that'll set things straight. At least I'll have time to think of what to say.

I pick up Leo. My leg crumbles under the added weight. Leo's heavy body falls on top of me. *I can do this. I can do this.* Sliding out from under Leo, I try again. The pain in my leg is so immense I can no longer feel it. It's like there's no leg there, just a weak support beam. I'm able to push Leo into the passenger's seat of the pickup. He flops down. Leg's dangling out of the car. I put the rest of him in, run over to the driver's side, and enter the truck, which is already running. I step on the gas and drive off into the night.

Please forgive me.

CHAPTER 30

THE FACTORY PART TWO

—

JAVIER JONES

DECEMBER 29, 2064

The purple sports car flees the scene. It heads off away from the factory, back into the white, ashy desert. Inside the car, two bodies.

Where's the third?

Running from behind the rock, Levi heads for the side door of the factory. I line up for the shot. The red tint falters, switching back to normal vision.

Why now? Sniper.

The Grim Reaper transforms into its sniper form. Looking through the scope, I pull the trigger. The first shot misses to the left. The red tint is back. Levi's about to enter the side door. As they open, I fire. It slices through the thick metal door. No body drops.

Shit!

The massive garage of the factory opens. The Wright Gang pours out. Some carry rifles, others melee weapons. Some ride out in large ATVs. Either way, it doesn't matter. Whatever they come at me with, they will lose. Red tint still on, I shoot down the yellow targets one group at a time. A large mass of them are on an electric buggy. The Grim Reaper takes out the driver. The buggy flips, killing a couple of riders. The rest are critically injured.

Mark yells, "I need a weapon!" snapping me out of my concentration.

"Then go grab one!" I yell back at him.

"But which one?" A lone soldier hides behind the ridge where Levi was. I shoot him through the head.

"Take his," I yell.

"I can't run out there! I'll get killed," he squeals.

I don't have time for this.

I get up and sprint toward the headless gang member. Switching the Grim Reaper back to an assault rifle build, I lay waste to the Wright Gang. About twenty attackers try to pick me off. Some sweep over from the right side on a caravan with their melee weapons. Bullets fly around me. I take one of the attackers and toss him into the line of fire. I shoot down the rest. Their yellow marks fade from my vision.

More attackers come from the front. They hide behind the ridge. One pops his head out to shoot. I kill him before he has time to pull the trigger. Another, same result.

Circle them.

I sneak around the ridge on the left side. One attacker shoots blindly toward my old location. He hits air. As I come around the ridge, the gang members all have their backs to me. I make quick work of them. Each receiving a shot in the back. I turn around to Mark. His face is covered in the blood of dead gang members. His eyes are wide and shaky.

"Take one and follow me inside," I say to him. He doesn't move. "Mark!" I bark. His eyes barely make contact with mine before looking back at the corpses. *Forget him.* I sprint toward the factory. More gang members approach on cars, hogs, and on foot. I shoot a group down approaching from my left. An attacker jumps onto my back. I flip him over and shoot him through the face.

Like a sonic boom, I'm knocked back. I fly through the air, weightless, and land with a bone-shattering thud. My ears ring. Blood trickles down my face. My red tint is gone.

What the hell was that?

I look up only to see a fiery golden shell flying toward me. Wide-eyed, I jump out of the way of the missile. The shock wave carries me through the air. As the ground approaches, I roll my body into a ball, so when I land, I bounce off my ass and land on a knee. Red tint back on, I locate the tank hiding inside the garage. Switching to an explosive shot, I pull, blowing up the tank and collapsing the wall holding the garage door. A second explosion, seconds after the first, sends the factory up in flames, adding a new light to the black night.

Levi.

"You all right?" Mark stands next to me with his hand extended. In his other hand, a rifle with an ax bayonet. He struggles to hold it up, his arm shaking. I reach out and grab his free hand, yanking myself up from the ground.

"He's this way," I grumble. Flipping a fallen buggy, I jump on and ride toward the burning factory, with Mark riding in the back. Another couple of gang members approach us, but we make short work of them. As soon as they disappear, my eyes switch back to normal view. *I think I'm starting to get the hang of this.* We arrive at the side door Levi entered. A gang member lies flat on the ground, a syringe jutting from his neck.

Poison. Can't even kill him quickly.

The open factory has a large open first floor. Assembly lines are filled with half-completed car frames, half-molded weapons, and scraps of bloodied armor. The left wall of the factory has collapsed down, with the backside of the tank sticking out of the rubble. To my right, a fire burns, consuming the back half of the factory. It jumps onto oily car frames and other machines, spreading rapidly. A staircase next to me leads to a wooden second level that wraps around the factory like a track. A couple of bridges connect the far sides together for quick access. Another body lies collapsed on the staircase with a syringe sticking out of his neck.

Gotcha.

As I sprint up the stairs, yelling comes from the first floor. A couple of gang members sprint at us, carrying wrenches and hammers. My eyes switch over to the red tint. "Deal with them!" I order Mark without missing a step. Gunfire outplays the crackling of the burning fires before quickly receding.

The second floor is nearly vacant. Only a few boxes and scorched bodies cover the wobbly wood floor. Further down, more men appear. "He went this way!" one screams. Chasing after them, I lock on to the six yellow targets. After a moment of sprints, I catch up. Another figure appears. His skinny frame jumps from a window before it burst into flames.

A nearly silent tick from above catches my ear. On the ceiling, a red flash erupts into a massive fire, consuming the six gang members a few feet ahead of me. The hair on my face burns from the flames. I fall back on the creaking floor, my face going numb from the pain. I roar and pat out the flames. They disappear. My body slowly loses its ability to feel. The burning sensation on my face is completely gone. *Neat trick.*

Where the explosion came from, a gaping hole has replaced it. The full moon looks in through it. The fire engulfs the entire second floor. The opposite side burns along with the first floor. The floor creaks as the foundation weakens.

"JJ," Mark whimpers from behind me. He takes a step forward, and the floor gives out under him. Mark screams and clings to the splintering floor. "JJ!" he yells. "Help!" In the distance, Wright Gang members scream as an explosion rocks the collapsing factory.

Found you.

I'm trapped inside this collapsing building. My skin blisters from the heat. There's no exit. Each window is surrounded by flames. The floor behind me is now completely gone. The only exit seems to be a hole in the roof twenty-four feet away. Behind the flames, a collapsed pillar on the far wall. As the roof caves in, I sprint toward it, barely avoiding the debris. I lower my shoulder and burst through the searing metal door.

Outside, the night is only lit by the full moon above and the fire behind me.

Where are you?

In the red tint, multiple yellow targets flee the factory, most on foot. One drives a motorcycle to the crushed garage. It exits and runs into the factory. As it disappears into the factory, a group fights over the bike. Beyond them, one yellow target struggles to drag another to my truck. Shutting off the red tint, I zoom in on the far away scuffle. It's Levi. He's dragging away an unconscious Leo. A needled syringe sticks out from his neck.

Not another life.

A motorcycle is parked far away from the burning factory. A couple of fleeing gang members fight over control of the bike.

Jumping down from the balcony, I switch to my red tint. Focusing on the gang members, I pull four shots. The yellow targets vanish from my sight. No other gang member approaches the bike. It's mine.

You won't ruin another life.

CHAPTER 31

LOVE OR LUST PART ONE: THE DOGS

MARK MORALES
DECEMBER 29, 2064

I land on the floor on my feet. *On my feet?* The building is no longer on fire. In fact, the night is quiet. The big wooden room has no windows, only a door, and a mirror. I can't see outside, but through the grooves in the log cabin's walls, bright light shoots through, filling the cabin with an orange glow. It's like twenty spotlights hit, pointing in no single direction.

The sudden bleating of sheep jolts me out of my trance. *Am I dead?* Walking over to the mirror, the sound of sheep gets louder. Their hoofs clop on the ground. There must be about a hundred.

The closer I get to the mirror, the harder it is for me to actually walk. My legs, tired. Standing, a chore. My back hurts with sharp pain. *Shit, I think I have to crawl.* As the thought appears in my mind, I drop to the ground like a rock. My legs instantly feel relief. My back is no longer in pain. My pace picks up. Crawling faster to the mirror, I freeze.

I am no longer a person but a sheep. White wool and all.
Yeah, I'm definitely dead.

Before I can even figure out what's up, the door swings open with a smack. No one there, but the door stays open like somebody's holding it.

If I leave, will I die? What? No. I'm a sheep right now. There's no way this is real.

Walking to the door, my head strains. My neck and head pull away from the door, but my legs churn forward. A tugging sensation around my head, as if pulled by a rope.

Stop being scared. Be a man and walk through the door.

My body aches, and my muscles are sore from my struggle. I am in a forest. Its night. In front of me, hundreds of sheep walk in a hurry, but not scared enough to run. They're bleating like crazy. Their big black eyes wild. Their bodies indistinguishable from the other. They all look exactly like me.

Over all the bleating, a loud, deep grunting noise comes from behind. I turn around only to be face-to-face with a pig. A giant, fat pig. It's a pinking brown, with a slimy and snot-filled nose. Drool drips from its giant tusks and slobbering mouth. The thing is so big it fills the entire cabin.

Where the hell did this thing come from?

The sheep stampede in random directions, scared of the pig. The sky is dark red. In the distance, fire burns down the forest. The smoke thickens, making it hard to breathe. The fire plows its way toward the flock, causing the sheep to frenzy even more. Before long, the sky is a mixture of bright orange, red, and dark purple.

Out of the fire come the dogs. They are beautiful. Some have dark brown coats, others like wolves. Barking in unison, they swarm, herding the panicking sheep into order. The sheep stumble over each other, trying to break their formation, but the dogs won't allow them. Flexing their power over the sheep, the dogs gain control.

Why couldn't I have been a dog?

As they continue to herd the sheep, one stares at me. A dark lab brown eyes full of anger and panic, but in complete control over itself. After a moment of eye contact, the dog moves on.

I face the pig.

Maybe if I act like the dog, I can scare away the pig.

I run at the pig and let out a pathetic bleat. The pig's lips crack and bleed into a smile. Laughing a deep, thundering chuckle, the pig jumps at me. My tiny sheep legs can't get out of the way fast enough. I'm in slow motion, and the pig's moving at two times the normal speed. I get slammed back and land with a solid thud in the middle of the herd, who babble and bleat in terror at the sight of me.

What the shit is going on?

I try to stand up only to be trampled by another sheep. Then another. Then another. It's like they don't even see me. A gap in the herd, I bolt. Dodging sheep after sheep, I make it to the edge of the flock. I turn around toward the cabin. The door is closed. The pig is gone.

Another dog, this one white with big blue eyes, barks at me. Without any control of my body, I jump back into the flock. The dog, no doubt happy with my scare, falls back into formation.

The sheep bleat like crazy. Eyes filled with panic. They bump into each other, sometimes knocking down one of their own. But instead of stopping to help, they just continue on, like they don't care. Some even trample the fallen sheep. Some are more aggressive than others. They try to break formation before being put back into place by the dogs.

As the forest burns around me, the sense of panic becomes too much. Some of the sheep begin to fight, tipping others over and messing up the flock. These sheep are just weak and mean. They don't care about each other and stumble on like they're nothing.

The brown dog from earlier joins the rest of the dogs and helps take out the bad sheep. The brown dog grabs one by the neck and drags it into the fire. The brown dog returns unscathed from the flames.

Are these dogs fireproof too?

Before long, I can see why the sheep are so panicky. Being forced through their path by the dogs and the fire around them, they are being led to a slaughterhouse. The pig is there, sitting on the roof, smiling at the meal he is about to enjoy.

The sheep panic when seeing the pig and his slaughterhouse. They bleat and run into each other. They sprint and stampede, trying to outrun the dogs, but the dogs are just too fast. They herd the sheep toward the slaughterhouse. The sheep that break out of the flock are too scared to run into the fire. Instead of taking the risk and jumping in, they join the stampeding flock.

Dream or not, I don't want to get eaten by that pig. There's got to be a way out of here.

Out of the corner of my eye is the brown dog about a hundred feet in front of me, no longer herding the sheep. He holds his stare for a moment before bolting into the fire, leaving the sheep and the rest of the dogs behind.

Am I supposed to follow him? Is that what he's saying?

As I reach the place the dog entered the fire, I see the pathway. He sits another hundred feet or so away. I bleat, happily knowing I have a way to escape the slaughter.

Jumping out of the flock, I run into the flames on the path the dog has set for me. Before I can catch him, the dog takes off. I chase after him, trying to keep up. My short stubby sheep legs can barely keep the dog in my sight. Before long, I lose him in the flames. Only the path where the dog went.

Shit, what if I lose him for good or fall too far behind. Will the flames come back in and burn me?

The flames burn my fur. My sheep skin blisters.

If only I can catch up to this damn dog.

With my eyes barely open, I see the end. The dog sits waiting for me. A large gap in the flames has been set up so that we can be safe. I reach another gear.

As I'm about to reach the dog, the ground changes from dirt to stone. The trees disappear, and all that's left is the night. I can't see anything in front of me. The dog has disappeared.

He went straight, so just go straight.

As I run, the ground beneath me vanishes, and I fall, scream-bleating, a raging river about five hundred feet below. I hit the river with a massive clap. The water freezing and cold. The current pushes me forward. I try swimming to the surface, but I don't know which way to go. I can't see anything in the dark water. My lungs burn.

So now I'm going to die as a sheep? Great.

The river pushes me up to the surface. My head bobs up and down in and out of the water, but I can breathe. At the top of the cliff is the dog. He stares at me but does nothing as I bleat for help. He turns back into the flames where he came from. I'm alone, cold, and dying, all because I decided to chase some damn dog out of a forest.

The river flows to a waterfall, and there's nothing I can do. My sheep legs can barely keep me afloat, let alone swim against a current. So I let the river take me. I fall.

Instead of landing in more water, I land on solid stone. My entire body is on fire like I'm being stabbed over and over again by hot blades. It's agonizing. I can't even scream anymore. I just sit there, waiting to die.

Why did that dog lead me here?
Why did I need to die?
What did I do to deserve this?
Why couldn't I just die like the rest of the sheep?
Mom was right. I can't trust anyone, no matter how nice they seem. I need to set my own path. The right path.

The stars in the orange and red sky above are beautiful as always. They kind of blend in. The moon, burning just as orange as the stars, is laughing at me. It has a cartoonish smile, laughing at me as if my pain is somehow funny.

The more I stare at the moon, the more it blinds me. My eyes are in agony but unable to look away.

Oh no. Please no more. I don't deserve this. I'm a good person. Please, no more. Just kill me already.

As the moon gets closer, the colors around me are overtaken by white.

I'm back in the old factory in Nowhere. I'm lying on the floor of the first story. The remains of the second story floor are all over the place. Despite the flames burning around me, I can't feel anything. I can still see the stars from the first floor. They are more covered now by some blurry object. As my vision focuses, the object becomes clearer. It's a face.

Mom?

CHAPTER 32

LOVE OR LUST PART TWO: FULL OF G.L.E.

LEVI O'SCANDRICK
DECEMBER 29, 2064

"You know he's going to kill you," Leo mocks in a drowsy voice. "His mind is already made up. I guarantee there's nothing either of us can do to stop that." He lies near motionless in the seat next to me. His body completely relaxed.

He can't be alive. Didn't see him die ...

"He's a Replacement," I say to Leo.

"Wow, you really are the smartest man in the world," he antagonizes. He laughs and smirks his contorted grin.

JJ was against the consciousness download. He never wanted that.

"Tell me, when he gets here, are you going to kill him, or am I going to force your hand? I crave the latter option! I feel like it would be so much more entertaining that way, wouldn't you agree?" I hit him with the butt of my gun, and blood pours from the open wound above his eye.

"Oh, there's that fight I'm dying to see," he says as blood drips from his forehead.

"You should choose your words more carefully," I threaten. He just grins.

I park the pickup about a mile away from the border fence, just out of sniper range. The week-long New Year's Celebration in Paradise City: New York lights the night sky purple. The barren desert surrounding the New York landscape matches the purple hue. The ash on the ground catching the color of the lights.

"Why do you want him? You want him to kill me? Make my death that much more miserable? And for what, a flash drive? For Marshall? Leo, he uses you for his dirty work and nothing more."

"You honestly think I care what happens to Saint Jimmy?" he says Marshall's name like it makes him nauseous. "See, I worked for that guy for the past twelve years of my life. I died eight times during that span. But I always returned. Do you know why Levi? Because I needed to teach these schemers—like Marshall, like Elani, like yourself—that with all their planning and all their craving to control us, our thoughts, and our imaginations, they still will never be anything more than a brick in their glorious wall. They will never outgrow the system that controls them.

"You see, all these people, in these cities, out in Nowhere, they're trying to find happiness in a world that refuses to allow it to exist. Now I know you have your happy place. I've heard you say it to yourself a thousand and a half times. But what good really does a fantasy do for you? What good does any part of this system do for you?"

Leo points behind me. In the distance, the sound of a motorbike fills the silent night.

Plan: JJ has no idea who he is anymore. He's become an extension of Leo. Show him home. Show him you still care. Show him that Leo is a sinister prick. Show him the truth.

"To beat the schemers, I was forced to become one," he continues, slowly gaining strength back in his voice. "Now, I only have one real goal. I have this insatiable craving to reset this world. To turn it on its head. Break it down to the dust we choke on in our sleep."

I've got to move now. Get my word out before Leo can manipulate him further.

"And now, I begin my plan with you," Leo finishes. He lunges at me, swinging a dagger at my neck. I dodge too slowly. The dagger cuts my cheek. The pain of the slice burns as warm blood drips out of the wound.

Leo grabs my neck and squeezes with his hands. His long fingernails dig into the skin. He raises the dagger to stab me. I punch him in the ribs, knocking him off balance.

His grip weakens as he falls back into the passenger seat. I kick him in the nose, which he promptly grabs.

Stuffing the pistol into my pants, I exit the truck. The night air pierces my skin, causing the hairs on my arms to stand. The purple lights from the annual New Year's Eve party inside PC:NY are so bright they light up the night sky a mile away, making the dust and ash piles that poof up around my feet purple clouds.

Leo is still sitting in the truck, holding his nose like a dog licking his wound.

"Get out," I yell at him.

"You're going to have to drag me out of this thing," he taunts.

Why does he have to be petty about it? Sighing, I open the door, greeted by a smiling Leo. A pocket-sized .22 aimed at my gut. Slamming the door, the bullet ricochets and penetrates Leo's leg, causing him to roar in agony.

"You mother fucker," he screams. "You shot me!"

What game is he playing?

"I didn't shoot you. Now get out."

"No!" he screams at the top of his lungs. "I won't let you kill me! Just look at what you've done already!" The roar of the motorcycle grows. Leo pulls up his tan button-down top to reveal the bullet wound in his hip, right next to a small screen that has vital signs of ..."

"You're JJ's host?" I ask.

"Oops, did I forget to mention that? It must have slipped my mind."

Taking a step back, I yell, "Shit!" and pace around aggressively.

That's it. He won! That motherfucker had this all planned out from the very beginning, and I fell for it like the absolute idiot I am. I can't do anything to him! I literally can't! If I kill him, JJ dies, but if I don't kill him, then JJ's mind slowly turns into Leo's.

Stick to the plan. That should hopefully get him thinking enough for his brain to break the rewrite, allowing me to become the host.

I approach the car breathing heavily. Leo still flashes the screen. Its blue light is bright, nearly blinding me. But as I get a closer look ... engraved on the top of the screen like a regrettable tattoo is G.L.E.'s smiling fucking moon. *Fucker has no idea. G.L.E.'s tech never mastered a complete takeover. It's a shared one where the two minds fight to be the dominant one. No matter what, JJ will have Leo in him, but now ...*

"Hey, what are you—Ahhhh!" I yank Leo out of the truck and slam him on the ground. I pin him to the ground, and I bash in his face with the butt of my gun. He just relishes in the moment, not even hesitating to let loose his full array of laughter and screams.

"You know why we chose him and not Aisling or Kaiya, or even Jackson?" Leo asks with his face covered in blood. "Because men are stupid. No matter how smart they think they are, they always think with the wrong head." He can barely finish the sentence without laughing.

Is he short-circuiting?

"You know," he says through his laughter, "by the time all this is over, you will die, JJ will die, and I will move onto my ninth life. And the best part about it, no one will know anything even happened all because of your little Pyramid. There's not a soul left on this planet that will even care to remember you and JJ. Like I said before, in the end, you'll fade into nothingness. Just another bland and boring cog in the machine."

I hit him again in the mouth for good measure. Unlike the other hits, he doesn't laugh. He just holds in his teeth as they fall out of his mouth.

The loud revving of a motorbike approaches, its single headlight sending a streak of yellow through the purple night.

All right. The stage is set. Just get him close.

JJ approaches. Carrying a large rifle in his hand, he hops off the bike. It skids and crashes into a dead tree, catching on fire. JJ's eyes are filled with a glassy-eyed intensity. Tears puddle on his bottom eyelid, clumping his eyelashes together in a way that makes him look like he's wearing mascara. His jaw protrudes forward, giving him an underbite. Although recognizable, his face is scarred, bloodied, and bruised. Random splotches of beard and charred hair line his once carefree face. His pupils dilated. He's holding a rifle in his left hand, Leo's dominant hand …

He's in a worse place than I thought. I need a new plan …

I jump behind Leo. With my leg wounded, it's more like I fall on top of him. JJ freezes. He holds his gun in his left hand. His body calm. His eyes stressless. *If he kills Leo, he becomes him. Leo will be in complete control. I can't let that happen.*

I push Leo behind me and guard him like JJ taught me to guard people in basketball. Arms up, legs wide. "You're not touching him." I try to say firmly, but my voice wavers. It cracks like I'm a thirteen-year-old going through puberty.

"Move or die," he responds. His voice is horse. His eyes glow red.

Military tech? He really made you into a monster.

Short and sweet. Every word counts.

"If you kill him, his consciousness will take over yours, killing you."

"JJ," Leo interrupts, "Remember what I told you."

"Your body will still exist," I continue, "but your brain will be Leo's."

"Do it, JJ!" he begs. "Please do it. Don't let him hurt you again!"

"That's how the transfer works. That's what the screen on his hip is for if you even considered questioning it. If you remove it—" Sharp, cold pain in my low back. The blade of a small knife twists in my kidney. My legs weaken. My body fails to maintain its strength. The accumulating injuries have finally caught up. *No. Not like this.*

Leo's knife and body are the only things supporting me. His free arm holds me up. My body lies against it.

"Why'd you do it, man," he whimpers. His eyes don't cry, but his face wrinkles like he is.

"Leo is messing with your mind," I somehow manage to say through the agonizing pain. "He's trying to manipulate you like he did to me."

"So you admit it?" he asks abruptly.

"What? Admit what?"

"You killed them to save your own skin," Leo says behind me through a mouth full of broken teeth.

"JJ, you don't need to kill him. Let's just get out of here and finish this somewhere else."

Leo's voice rings in my head, *"His mind is already made up. I guarantee there's nothing either of us can do to stop that."*

"No!" JJ yells, "I need him to admit it. Say it!" Through my fading peripheral vision, Leo smiles. He's turned JJ into his monster. He won.

Not if he kills me. If I can plant a seed ...

"We were happy!" I yell at him, a sudden wave of energy propels me off Leo. "I had everything I ever wanted. I had a family. We were a family. You, me, Kaiya, Aisling ... Jackson." His eyes don't soften when he hears their names. Not a good sign.

"I had people I could rely on, and now he's here breaking us apart because Marshall wanted to keep his precious secret in the dark. But I don't know what else there is for me to do, JJ. I don't know how else I can clear his manipulation from your mind. Will killing me do it? Will that make you see things clearly?"

His dilated eyes are emotionless. He looks back at Leo, then back to me. I can't get a read on him.

I continue, "Look, I've lived my life running from my problems and not taking responsibility for my actions. And look where that's gotten me? You don't have to do that, JJ. Learn from my mistakes. Be better than me. Just don't listen to him."

He looks at Leo. Their eyes lock. *I can't let him win.* JJ raises his gun. I push Leo away as JJ shoots. A cold sensation in my chest. Looking down, a hole right under my collar bone. My legs weaken. I collapse. The pain dissipates along with all feeling. A plume of ash floating above me.

JJ's emotionless eyes now express worry. He turns toward PC:NY, then back to me. *C'mon. Just get the words out.* "Be better," I'm able to mumble. As blood floods my lungs, my greatest regret walks away. He picks up Leo and puts him into the pickup. They drive off, back into Nowhere. Hopefully, he can find a better life.

My vision blurs. Black spots cover the fading image of JJ placing Leo into the pickup.

I've imagined this day so many times in my head, but I never thought it would end so lonely.

Am I worth it? A purple moon comes into view in the same colored sky. It smiles, encouraging me to come with it. *Wait ... is that the G.L.E. logo? Of course, they sponsor the afterlife.* In a bright purple flash, I end up standing at the line that divides me from my family. Jackson now runs around the now purple-tinted picnic table. Kaiya feeds a baby girl some apple sauce. *I have a daughter now?*

Then, four more people enter the scene. Ali and Janet hold hands and take their seats on the left side of the table. Ali's his typical perky, and Janet even manages to crack an unfiltered smile. Kaiya embraces with a bear hug. Aisling walks out of the trees, looking as flamboyant as ever. *Of course, she has to dress fancy for a picnic.* She is followed closely by JJ, looking like his old self again. His clean and boyish charm and attitude are magnetic. Jackson runs up to him and tackles him to the ground. JJ laughs and does the best possible thing, laughing as he asks me, "What you doing over there, numb-nuts?"

"Hey," Kaiya barks at him. "No cussing in front of the kids."

"I don't think numb-nuts is a cuss word," Janet says.

"Of course you don't," Kaiya teases lightheartedly.

"Wait," Jackson says, his brow furrows tightly like he's trying telepathy again. "What are numb-nuts?" Everyone blurts out laughing. With each chuckle, my shoulders relax, and the stress exits my body. But as I'm about to take my step over that line, I freeze.

Am I worth it? Have I done enough to earn it?

A tugging in my chest paralyzes me with my foot an inch above the line. As I stand there, waiting to take a step over that barrier into my paradise, I can't help but think of that infamous line, "The worst way to die is when you're lying on your deathbed and, looking back at your life, realizing you lived a life full of regret, and knowing there's nothing you can do to change it."

I failed JJ. He's lost, in the arms of the devil, and there's nothing I can do to change that. I tried my best to be a better person. One good deed at a time. But was it enough? Do I deserve this ending?

No. Stop. Have some faith and breathe. I have my loving wife, my son, and a daughter I'm dying to meet. I have my friends with me, along with ones I've never imagined myself meeting, let alone befriending. Smile. Everything is going to be all right.

I take the step.

CHAPTER 33

LOVE OR LUST PART THREE: THE BLEEDING ROSE

JAVIER JONES
DECEMBER 29, 2064

Leo sits next to me silently. He struggles to put his teeth back into his mouth. He fumbles around like a weasel.

Be better.

Levi deserved this. I mean, he did, right? Yeah, he definitely did. There's no room for people like him in this country anymore. There can't be. Otherwise, we'll be stuck in this terrible place forever. It was the right decision. And knowing him, he's probably still alive, trying to break into San Francisco or something like that.

Be Better.

Such cheesy lines to be stuck in my head. I mean, for a final breath, you've gotta come up with something better than that. I bet that girl can come up with something better than that. Where has she been?

"Who is that girl?" I ask.

Leo's eyes widen before returning to fixing his teeth. "What girl?"

"I keep seeing this beautiful girl, this woman, in my head, and she just seems so familiar. Who is she?" I stammer. The more questions I ask, the more pain shoots through my brain. Flashes of white.

Here we are again, this time lying in a jean-colored bed. Waves crash outside the window of our first-floor bedroom. The woman is writing something in her notebook. Walking over to me, she climbs into bed and sits within an inch of my face. The hairs of my neatly trimmed beard stand up as her breath hits my neck.

"Cuz life isn't always flowers and snowflakes," she says quietly, "sometimes it's roses."

"I don't get it," I respond like the genius I am.

The woman drops the notebook on the bed. "What's not to get?" she asks, flustered. Her hazel eyes focused on mine. "Aren't roses flowers?"

"Yeah …"

"So I don't get it. Why sometimes say it's roses when roses are flowers?"

"You really don't get it?" she asks, stunned, as if it should be obvious.

"No. I don't."

"Don't worry. I'll teach it to you some time."

"Aka, you don't get what it means either."

She scoffs and gently slaps my chest and says, "Shut up." She cuddles next to me, laying her head on my chest.

"Gimme a break. I just came up with it."

"I'm kidding, I'm kidding," I say jokingly. "It's beautiful. I'm sure some dumbass somewhere will find something to say about it." For a second, her warm hazel eyes study mine.

Something catches my eye. Out the window is a face. Its cartoonish smile and look remind me of the Saturday morning cartoons I got to watch as a kid. Its body is nonexistent. Instead, the face lies on the pink moon in the sky. A warm, tingling sensation fills my chest. I look back at my Aisling's warm hazel eyes. With the pink moon lighting the room, the scene is too perfect. As I lean in for a kiss, I'm met with the soft, cuddly smack of a pillow. We both laugh as the dream fades away.

Leo's beady eyes squint as if examining me under a microscope. The electric blue screen on his hip lights up through his bloodied shirt. "What is that thing anyway? Is that what Levi was talking about?" I ask.

"Wow, look at you, asking so many questions," Leo says, teasing me. "You never were so curious about things before."

"Why don't you just answer the question?" I fire back.

Where did this come from? The more I question him, the more pain my head's in. It's that stupid screen thing.

"Look, Javier," he says dismissively. "You're the soldier. I tell you where to go, and you go. If something is necessary for change, I'll let you know, and there you go. It's a pretty system. Worked so far, right? We got rid of that creep and scum sucker. And we're just getting started."

As if a dam bursts, memories flood my brain. Levi and Kaiya are in the hospital while Kaiya's in labor. Levi introduces me to Aisling, who … Oh shit. She's the girl.

Be better.

Ahead is a wooden tree leaning against a broken house. A large branch sticks over the road, right at penetrating level. Leo rambles on about some nonsense, his words washed out by thought.

Be better.

I've turned into the monster. Leo broke me. He beat me. He made me kill someone I loved. And Aisling … if she's still out there. Stop thinking, I tell myself. Just go.

Slamming my foot on the break, Leo flies out of the truck. He lands on the pavement with a solid thud. Although I'm not wounded, my chest is hollow. My eyes are heavy.

Oh shit, Levi was right. He can't die. He lies on the ground, wounded but alive. "You idiot," he whimpers, "You don't have a plan. You can't. Once I die, you will—"

I step on Leo's chest and grab an arm. The Wright Gang are the worst, but they had one good idea. Pulling as hard as I can, I rip off Leo's right arm. He roars in agony. "No," he pleads, "you can't fall for his manipulation. You can't—" I rip off the other arm.

Leo's screen flashes "New Host Recommended." The screen on his hip tears off with a bloody yank. Wires flail around as I pull. My vision is blue. There's a socket on my hip I can plug it into. Slapping the screen onto it, my vision goes black. Although my body moves, I cannot see what is happening. An intense heat comes from behind me, singeing the hairs on my neck.

The longer I'm blind, the better I feel. My head no longer aches. The pain in my body gone. My mind removed from a cloud—a fog—I didn't even know was there.

And with a flash, my vision returns. I'm standing a couple of feet away from the now burning car. In the deep purple night, I find myself staring at a tattoo on my left forearm. It's a rose, with its thorns piercing my arm, making me bleed. Above me, the pink moon burns a hole through the purple night. Like a beacon, it encourages me to follow it back toward the factory. As my shy smirk turns to a genuine giggle, I say to myself, "Dumbass," and walk off into the purple night, leaving behind my burning past in the hopes of finding a girl I don't even know exists.

EPILOGUE

JANET SIMS

DECEMBER 30, 2064

Levi's body lies on the ash. The purple sky and ground match the coloring of the Good Life. Why he sent me away instead of keeping us here to help him, it's stupid. It made no sense. His hero complex got the best of him. For such a smart guy, he really was bad at making life choices.

His old features finally look relaxed. His neck has no veins popping out of it. His eyes are closed. He looks peaceful like he's finally gotten to sleep. *If only they knew. If only they knew how amazing he actually was. Crazy, sure. About as pessimistic and stubborn as they come, but good at heart.*

"Is he ..." Ali asks as he exits the Good Life. His legs are healed. Or fixed, I guess? Levi must've known what he was doing because he sent us to a mechanic's shop. Now, Ali walks like nothing even happened.

"Yeah," I respond, a lump blocking my words. I can't help it. I hated him for so much of my life. He was the reason we have two worlds. He is the reason the P.R.R.C. still controls us. I pull out the flash drive. *If only they knew.*

"So I don't know how you do it out here," I tell Ali, "but we bury the dead."

"We do that too," he says, his eyes still focused on Levi.

"So, where should we do it?" I ask.

In the distance, yellow lights flash in the purple night. It's the truck from before. The one on the cliff. The ones who shot Ali. Who killed Levi. *They've come back for him. They're not getting him.*

"Janet, let me handle them. I could use this to test my new leg joints out."

"No," I answer forcefully. Ali looks back at me, confused. "No?"

"They're mine."

Okay, car. How do you work? I place my hand on the cold purple steel. It sends shivers through my body. How did Levi do this? How did he get those guns out? *Maybe it's like Circe?* "Hey, Good Life, give me all the guns you've got." The car responds with a satisfying ding. Out of the hood come two massive black machine guns, the side of the car another, two from behind, and a massive gatling gun from the hood. *Wow, Levi really doesn't mess around.*

The black pickup rolls to a stop. The bumper of the car falls off as it stops. Out of the truck steps a man in a large black duster. His wild light brown hair sticks out in every direction. His tan skin absorbs the purple light of the city. His beard is charred. His face scarred. His brown eyes watering. Seeing Levi's body, he collapses.

"I'm sorry," he weeps. "I'm so sorry." He can't control himself as he violently cries. Ali relaxes. His fists at his side. *He's not really buying this act?*

"Hey!" I yell at the man. "You have five seconds to get the fuck out of here! If you don't, I'll end you! You understand me?"

"I didn't," he whimpers, "If only I'd known."

Why does he look familiar? Eerily familiar. Oh shit ...

"You're Javier Jones."

"Who?" Ali asks.

"Levi's friend," I answer. That can't be right. There's no way he would hunt Levi. It must've been a look-alike. No, that doesn't make sense. Why is he here? If he's alive, is Aisling? Is Kaiya? And Levi's kid?

"Oh, if he's Levi's friend," Ali says, "then he's our friend to ... wait ... You're the guy who shot me!" Ali runs at Javier.

"No, Ali, wait!" He ignores my plea and jump-kicks Javier in the face. Surprisingly, it does nothing. Jones's face doesn't show any wound or stress. He stares at Levi, his eyes wide and watering. Ali freezes, staring at Jones in disbelief.

What the hell? No one's ever taken a hit by Ali and not even budged! What is he?

Javier stands, "I'm sorry for everything I've done to you both." His voice is shaky and frail. Each word said through a whimper, "I'm sorry I shot you. The, uh, easy way to explain it is I wasn't myself. But that's changed. I ain't here looking for a fight. I'm here for Levi. I want to have a funeral for my friend. Then," he turns to the city, "Imma destroy Marshall. Imma rip his spine from his body and beat him with it. Him and all his pets. I don't care what it costs. But I need to do this."

"Um, that's great, but we don't really trust you," Ali says, "because, you know, you shot me. And Levi would like that I don't trust you."

"Because you're naïve," Javier says in a matter-of-fact tone.

Ali's eyes widen, "What? How'd you—"

"I've know Levi for twenty-something years. I know what he probably said about all of you." He studies me for a moment, "I'm guessing too pretty. Can't handle herself? Maybe even petty?"

"That's none of your—. No, you know what? Good Life guns."

Jones raises his hands, "How about we burry him first? At least that's something we can both agree needs to be done."

"Fine," I say bitterly, "but one wrong move, and you're toast. And roll up your sleeves. You're digging." I look at Ali, who nods his head, impressed.

***

"You remind me a lot of him," Javier says, standing next to me.

"I don't know whether that's an insult or a compliment," I tease.

He laughs softly. "Yeah, neither do I. He was strange like that."

Levi's grave isn't anything special. It's next to a burnt tree. A destroyed motorcycle as his tombstone. *He deserved better than this.*

Jones wipes the dirt off his hands. His eyes don't move from the grave. "I know you don't trust me because—"

"You shot Ali and killed Levi" I interrupt.

"Right, but hear me out. The guy who did this to me made me do those things. He's gone now. He used this." He pulls up his shirt, revealing a blue screen with his vital signs. "He gave me fake memories of Aisling … I don't even know if she's alive. I have to find her. But this guy, he's gone. Like Permanently. At least, I think. If not, then he's probably in this Paradise City. You don't have to trust me. You don't even have to like me, but I want the same thing as you. I want to destroy Marshall and all his allies. So, can we put away the hate and try to work together? Please."

I can't get myself to trust him. He's different than the brief moment I saw him. He's calmer, less likely to rampage.

"No, I can't. No matter what you say, you're still the guy who did these horrible things."

"So was Levi," Ali says, sitting on the hood of the Good Life. "You said the same things about him. Isn't it kind of funny you're doing it to his friend now? Ironic, right?" his brow burrows as he tries to figure out if he used the word correctly. "Right?"

I don't know if Ali can even fight him. That kick ... If he can't, this car is loaded with weapons. I don't think anyone can survive an encounter with it. And if he does something stupid, I'll get to kill him.

"Fine," I say, "but you ride in the back."

Javier looks intently at the purple sky, his brown eyes gentle and warm like he's falling in love with the scene. A contorted smile grows on his beaten tan face as one side of his mouth rises to a smile while the other tries to fight it. "Sweet! You won't regret this!" Ali enters the car, sitting shotgun. Jones begins to walk over the Good Life. I grab him. His arms are cold and hard like metal.

"You may be coming with us, Javier—"

"JJ, please," he interrupts.

"Fine, whatever. You may be coming with us. You may have Ali believing in you, but I don't trust you. Not for a second. You still pulled that trigger. Whatever b.s. excuse you have, I don't care. You're still the one who killed Levi O'Scandrick." I storm off before he can answer. Entering the Good Life, I start the car. *If worse comes to worst, this car is a bomb. I could trap him in here and blow it up.*

"All right," Ali says, grinning. "This is fun. We're having fun! How about we go back to my old camp? Show JJ what's on the flash drive."

"What flash drive?" JJ asks, scrunched up in the back seat, his knees at his chin.

No. Not yet. I can't trust him yet. How about a test.

"I have a better idea," I say, looking at the purple halo that hovers above PC:NY's glorious wall. "Does anyone here know how to broadcast a message?"

Made in the USA
Columbia, SC
30 November 2022